SOUP AND APPETIZER

C·O·O·K·B·O·O·K

GOLDEN APPLE PUBLISHERS

SOUP AND APPETIZER COOKBOOK

A GOLDEN APPLE PUBLICATION/
PUBLISHED BY ARRANGEMENT WITH OTTENHEIMER PUBLISHERS INC.

JUNE 1986

GOLDEN APPLE IS A TRADEMARK OF GOLDEN APPLE PUBLISHERS

ISBN 0-553-19854-8

Contents

Stocks and Croutons   5

Fruit and Cheese Soups   12

Meat and Poultry Soups   16

Seafood Soups   25

Vegetable Soups   30

Cheese and Egg Appetizers   55

Meat and Chicken Appetizers   62

Nuts and Dips   68

Seafood Appetizers   73

Vegetable Appetizers   85

Equivalent Measures   94

Index   95

Stocks and Croutons

Brown Stock

2 to 3 pounds veal bones	5 quarts water
2 to 3 pounds meaty beef bones (including a bone with marrow)	10 peppercorns
	2 bay leaves
2 pounds of lean beef, in one piece for boiled beef or cut into pieces	8 to 10 sprigs of parsley
	1 sprig of thyme (or ¼ teaspoon dried thyme)
3 to 4 onions, unpeeled, or 2 onions and 2 leeks	Salt and pepper
	A few mushroom stalks or peelings
4 carrots	

Get butcher to break bones. Put them into a pan with beef and a little beef marrow or good dripping. Heat pan; as the bones and meat brown, stir and keep from burning. Remove; keep warm while browning vegetables. Return bones and meat to pan; cover with water. Add herbs, salt, pepper, and mushroom peelings or stems if available.

Bring to a boil. Skim frequently during the first hour. Then cover pan; simmer for 2 to 3 hours, by which time stock should be well flavored and a good brown color. (If meat is a large piece and is to be used as boiled beef, this can be removed after 2 hours and stock simmered without it for remaining cooking time).

Strain stock; let cool. Then skim off fat, which will form a crust on top. If stock is not required for a day or two, do not remove fat until just before using, as it acts as a protective seal. Keep in refrigerator or freezer.

Beef Stock

3	pounds beef brisket	1	large onion, studded with
2	pounds medium soup		10 cloves
	bones	1	celery stalk and leaves
5	quarts water	2	tablespoons salt
4	green onions and tops		

Place beef and bones in large baking pan. Bake at 400°F about 1 hour or until well browned on both sides. Remove from pan; place in a large stockpot. Drain off fat from baking pan; add 1 cup water to pan and scrape up brown bits from bottom. Pour into stockpot. Add remaining water and remaining ingredients except salt. Bring slowly to a boil, removing froth as it accumulates on surface. Cover and simmer 1 hour. Add salt. Simmer 3 hours longer.

Remove meat and vegetables. Strain through wet muslin. Chill; remove fat before using.

Chicken Stock

1	(4-pound) hen	6	green onions with tops
1	pound chicken wings	4	large carrots, quartered
2	tablespoons salt	2	stalks celery with leaves,
4	peppercorns		cut in 2-inch pieces
5	quarts water	1	large onion, studded with
½	bay leaf		3 cloves
Pinch of thyme			

Place chicken, salt, peppercorns, and water in a stockpot. Bring to boil over medium heat, removing scum from surface. Cover pot; reduce heat. Simmer 1 hour, skimming frequently. Add remaining ingredients; cover and cook about 2 hours and 30 minutes.

Skim off fat; season to taste with additional salt and pepper. Remove chicken and vegetables from stock. Strain stock through wet muslin. Chill and remove fat before using.

Cheese Soup

Fish Stock

½ to 1 pound fish backbones and skins (sole, turbot, or halibut)
1 onion, sliced
2 small carrots, sliced
2 stalks celery

6 sprigs of parsley
1 bay leaf
1 sprig of thyme
6 to 7 cups water
1½ cups white wine or cider (optional)
Salt and pepper

Put fish backbones and skins in a pan with sliced onion, carrot, celery, herbs, and water. Add white wine or cider if available. Then add salt and pepper. Bring very slowly to a boil; simmer 30 to 40 minutes, until liquid has reduced and is well flavored. Strain; cool. Use at once; or freeze for later use.

Vegetable Stock

3 medium-sized onions, unpeeled	2 to 3 quarts water
3 medium-sized carrots, peeled	6 peppercorns
2 leeks, white part only	1 bay leaf
4 to 5 stalks of celery	4 to 6 sprigs of parsley
1 small turnip, peeled	1 sprig of thyme (or ¼ teaspoon dried thyme)
1 tablespoon butter or oil	Salt and pepper

Cut up vegetables; brown these until golden in either a little butter or oil. Add water, herbs, and seasoning. Bring to a boil; simmer for 1-1/2 to 2 hours, by which time the stock should be well flavored. Strain; cool. Use for soups or sauces calling for vegetable stock.

White Stock

2 pounds raw veal knuckle bones	1 small sprig thyme (or ¼ teaspoon dried thyme)
1 chicken carcass and giblets	2 teaspoons salt
2 onions, peeled and sliced	6 peppercorns
2 carrots, peeled and sliced	1 small piece of mace
3 stalks of celery	3 quarts water
1 bay leaf	Rind of ½ lemon
6 sprigs of parsley	

Have butcher chop raw veal bones and chicken carcass into small pieces. Put these and giblets into pan of water with vegetables, herbs, and seasoning. Bring to a boil; skim frequently for about half an hour. Add 1 cup cold water; skim again. Add lemon rind; simmer 2 hours.

Strain through muslin and sieve; then let cool. Remove fat from the top. Use at once; keep in covered bowl in refrigerator or freezer.

Cheese Croutons

2 to 3 slices white bread
2 tablespoons butter
    (approximately)
A little mustard or vegetable
    extract

4 to 6 tablespoons grated
    Italian cheese
Salt and pepper
Cayenne pepper

Toast bread slices on 1 side only. Let cool. Then butter reverse side; spread with a little mustard. Sprinkle thickly with grated cheese and a little salt and pepper. Broil until cheese is melted and browned. Sprinkle with cayenne pepper. When slightly cooled, cut into squares or fingers. Serve hot. Makes 4 servings.

Greek Lemon Soup

Cream of Chicken Soup

Fried Bread Croutons

2 large slices white bread	**Salt and pepper**
Oil	**Onion powder to taste**
1 tablespoon butter	

Remove crusts from slices of bread; cut bread into small cubes. Heat enough oil in frying pan to come at least half way up the sides of bread cubes while cooking. When the oil is hot, add butter. When melted and foaming, add all bread cubes at once. Cook over a moderate-to-hot flame; stir constantly to ensure that cubes brown evenly.

When golden brown, place on kitchen paper to drain. Remove from pan when slightly less brown than final color you want, as they continue to cook for a few seconds because of hot oil.

Season with salt, pepper, and onion powder, if this will improve soup for which croutons are intended. Keep hot and serve separately. Makes 4 servings.

Bacon Croutons

2 slices bacon	**Pepper**
Oil	
2 large slices white bread, cut into cubes	

Remove rinds from bacon slices; chop the bacon finely. Put into a dry frying pan; cook slowly to extract fat, then cook until crisp and golden. Remove bacon bits; reserve.

Add enough oil to bacon fat to cook diced bread in same way as Fried Bread Croutons. When golden brown, remove; drain. Add bacon bits with pepper and serve hot. Makes 4 servings.

Fruit and Cheese Soups

Swiss Cherry Soup

½ cup seedless raisins	2 cups sliced fresh peaches, peeled
¼ cup lemon juice	½ cup honey
1 2-inch stick cinnamon	Salt to taste
6 slices navel orange	2 tablespoons cornstarch
5 thin slices lemon	¼ cup cold water
3 cups water	Yogurt for garnish
2 cups pitted dark sweet cherries, fresh or frozen	

Combine raisins, lemon juice, cinnamon stick, orange, and lemon slices. Add to water in a saucepan. Bring to a boil over medium heat. Reduce heat. Cover and simmer for 15 minutes. Remove cinnamon stick. Add cherries, peaches, honey, and salt to soup mixture. Bring to a boil.

Blend cornstarch and cold water. Stir into soup. Bring to a boil, stirring until soup is clear, about 2 or 3 minutes. Remove from heat.

Pour into a covered bowl and cool for several hours. Serve with yogurt. Makes 4 to 6 servings.

Danish Apple Soup

5 **medium-sized apples, unpeeled and quartered**	¼ **cup cold water**
½ **teaspoon lemon peel, grated**	½ **cup white wine**
	½ **cup sugar**
2 **tablespoons cornstarch**	1 **teaspoon cinnamon**

Simmer apples and grated lemon rind in water 15 minutes. Strain. Dissolve cornstarch in the cold water. Add to apple mixture, stirring constantly until clear. Add wine, sugar, and cinnamon. Simmer 5 minutes. Serve hot or cold. Makes 4 servings.

Pavian Soup

Cheese Soup

1 onion, finely chopped	1 egg yolk
1 tablespoon margarine	⅓ cup crème fraîche or sour
3 tablespoons flour	cream
4 cups broth	Shredded celery
1¼ cups grated cheese	Chopped parsley

Sauté onion in margarine. Stir in flour when onion has become transparent. Cover with broth, stirring constantly, and simmer for 5 to 6 minutes.

Stir in cheese and let it melt. It should not, however, be allowed to boil. Remove pot from heat; stir in egg yolk and crème fraîche or sour cream. Serve immediately garnished with celery and parsley. Makes 4 servings.

Greek Lemon Soup

2 quarts Chicken Stock (see Index)	3 eggs, separated
⅓ cup long-grain rice, rinsed	2 tablespoons lemon juice

Pour stock into 4-quart saucepan; bring to a boil. Reduce heat; simmer 5 to 10 minutes. Add rice; cook 15 to 20 minutes or until rice is tender. Remove from heat; cool slightly.

Beat egg yolks until thick and lemon colored, then add egg whites. Beat until foamy, adding lemon juice slowly and beating constantly.

Pour 1/2 cup of the broth into egg mixture very slowly, beating constantly to keep foamy, then beat in 1-1/2 cups broth gradually. Pour egg mixture slowly into remaining broth in saucepan, stirring constantly. Reheat slowly but do not boil. Serve immediately. Makes 6 servings.

Orange Soup

1 tablespoon cornstarch	¼ cup sugar
4 cups water	Whipped cream for garnish
1½ cups orange juice	Thin orange slice for garnish

Mix cornstarch in 1/4 cup of cold water. Bring rest of water to a boil. Add cornstarch mixture to boiling water to thicken slightly. Add orange juice and sugar. Serve either hot or cold, garnished with a spoonful of whipped cream and a thin orange slice.

Note: For a pudding, rather than a soup, add more cornstarch to thicken. Makes 6 servings.

Quick Bouillabaise

Meat and Poultry Soups

Beef Shank Supper Soup

4 **pounds meaty beef shanks, cut 1½ inch thick**	1 **tablespoon oregano**
1 **large onion, finely chopped**	1 **bay leaf**
2 **stalks celery, finely chopped**	1½ **teaspoons salt**
	6 **cups water**
1 **(1¾-pound) can whole tomatoes**	½ **cup pearl barley**
	4 **large carrots, cut in 1-inch chunks**
1 **teaspoon thyme**	1 **(10-ounce) package frozen cut beans**
¼ **teaspoon cloves**	1 **cup parsley, chopped**

In large soup kettle, brown meat in its own fat over medium heat. Remove and set aside. Add onion and celery to drippings in kettle. Sauté until onion is tender. Add tomatoes. Stir in seasonings and water. Add meat and bring to a boil. Reduce heat. Simmer, covered, for 1-1/2 hours. Remove meat from broth.

Refrigerate broth and skim fat from top. Trim meat, discarding fat and connective tissue. Return meat and bones with marrow to kettle. Heat to simmer. Add barley, carrots, and beans. Cook, uncovered, for 50 minutes or until beans are tender. Add parsley and salt to taste. Makes 6 servings.

New England Clam Chowder

Goulash Soup

2	tablespoons butter	2	tablespoons whole-wheat flour
1½	cups onions, finely chopped	1½	cups potatoes, cubed
2	cups red and green sweet peppers, cubed	1	cup cabbage, thinly sliced
2	teaspoons garlic, finely chopped	1	(1-pound) can tomatoes
1	tablespoon caraway seeds	4	cups water
2	tablespoons paprika	1	pound beef bones
2	tablespoons soy sauce	2½	cups leftover beef, cut into ¾-inch pieces

Melt butter in a large saucepan. Add onions and peppers. Sauté until tender but not soft. Add minced caraway and garlic to onions and pepper. Sprinkle with paprika. Stir in soy sauce and flour. Simmer for 5 minutes, stirring constantly.

Add potatoes, cabbage, tomatoes, water, meat, and bones. Simmer 45 minutes. Remove bones and serve. Makes 8 to 10 servings.

Chicken and Ham Soup

4 to 5 cups of clear chicken stock (or consommé)	1 tablespoon parsley, chopped
1 glass white wine	1 to 1½ tablespoons gelatin for cold soup
2 slices of mild ham	
½ cup fresh peas, lightly cooked	
1 teaspoon fresh tarragon, chopped, or ½ teaspoon dried	

If serving hot, heat clear chicken stock, adding at last minute a glass of white wine, shredded ham that has had all fat removed, and lightly cooked green peas and herbs. Serve hot. Sprinkle with chopped parsley.

If serving cold and using chicken stock that is not already jellied, put gelatin to soak in 1/2 cup of stock. When it has swollen, heat gently; add to heated stock. Skim off any grease carefully; add white wine; let cool in a bowl. When it is on point of setting, add shreds of ham and peas; spoon into soup cups. Chill well; serve garnished with chopped parsley or watercress leaves. Makes 4 to 6 servings.

Ham Chowder

2 cups potatoes, pared and diced	1 teaspoon salt
¼ cup celery, very finely chopped	1½ cups boiling water
	3 cups milk
¼ cup onion, very finely chopped	1½ cups ham, finely chopped
	¼ cup unsifted flour
	¼ cup water

Cook potatoes, celery, and onion in boiling salted water until tender. Add milk and ham. Heat to simmering.

Mix flour and 1/4 cup water. Stir into milk mixture. Cook, stirring occasionally, until thickened. Makes 6 servings.

Cod Soup with Orange

Chicken Gumbo

3 tablespoons butter or bacon fat
1 large or 2 smaller onions, chopped
1½ cups canned tomatoes, chopped
½ green pepper, seeded and chopped
¾ to 1 cup canned okra (or ready-cooked okra)
2 tablespoons rice
4 to 5 cups strongly flavored chicken stock made with whole chicken

1 to 2 cups cooked chicken, chopped
1 tablespoon parsley, chopped
1 teaspoon tarragon, chopped
½ cup cooked corn (optional)

Garnish
Fried Bread Croutons (see Index)

Melt butter or bacon fat in a soup pot; cook onion gently 5 to 6 minutes with lid on, until tender but not brown. Add chopped tomatoes, chopped pepper, okra, and rice. Pour in stock; mix thoroughly. Add salt and pepper if necessary. Cover pan; simmer until vegetables are tender, about 20 to 30 minutes.

Adjust seasoning; add chopped cooked chicken and herbs. If available, 1/2 cup of cooked corn can also be added. Reheat; serve hot. This soup can be served on its own as a main course; it is nice to serve Fried Bread Croutons (see Index) or thick bread and butter with it. Makes 4 to 6 servings.

Cream of Chicken Soup

4 cups Chicken Stock (see Index)
2 cups celery, finely chopped
1 small clove of garlic, pressed
¾ cup half-and-half

Salt and freshly ground white pepper to taste
2 cups cooked chicken, minced
½ cup Parmesan cheese, finely grated

Pour stock into a large saucepan; bring to a boil. Add celery and garlic; simmer 10 minutes or until tender. Pour into a blender container and process until pureed; return to saucepan.

Add cream, salt, and pepper; bring just to boiling point. Stir in chicken and cheese; heat, stirring, until cheese is melted and soup is well blended. Serve in soup bowls. A dash of whipping cream may be poured into center of each serving, if desired. Makes 8 servings.

Pavian Soup

4	**slices white bread**	**4**	**eggs**
3	**tablespoons butter, melted**	**6**	**tablespoons Parmesan**
5	**cups Chicken Stock (see**		**cheese, shredded**
	Index) or 2 (13-ounce)		
	cans regular strength		
	chicken broth		

Trim crusts from bread. Brush on both sides with melted butter; place on a cookie sheet. Bake at 350°F 30 minutes, or until golden. Pour stock into a large shallow saucepan; heat to boiling.

Reduce heat to low, then break eggs 1 at a time into a saucer; slide into liquid. Poach lightly. Remove with a slotted spoon and keep warm. Strain stock. Return stock to pan and heat to boiling. Put 1 toasted bread slice in each soup bowl. Top with 1 poached egg. Ladle soup over egg.

Sprinkle each bowl with 1-1/2 tablespoons of cheese and serve. Makes 4 servings.

Savory Shrimp Soup

Chicken Giblet Soup

2 sets of chicken giblets	Salt
1 large onion	Chicken cube (optional)
2 to 3 carrots	2 tablespoons butter
2 to 3 stalks celery	1½ tablespoons flour
Chicken skin and carcass (if available)	
5 cups water	*Garnish*
4 to 5 parsley stalks, 1 sprig of thyme, 1 bay leaf, tied together	2 chicken livers
	1 tablespoon butter
6 peppercorns	2 tablespoons parsley, chopped

Wash chicken giblets, removing livers. Reserve for garnish.

Peel onion; slice onion, carrots, and celery. Put into pan with giblets—and any skin or carcass from the chicken. Add water, herbs, peppercorns, and some salt. Bring slowly to a boil, skimming off any froth that rises to top. Reduce heat and simmer 1 to 1-1/2 hours, until vegetables are tender and giblets well cooked. Taste soup; if not well flavored, a chicken cube can be added. (Remove skin and carcass, or strain soup into another pan.)

Melt 2 tablespoons butter; blend in flour. Strain onto chicken stock; blend thoroughly. Bring to a boil, stirring constantly. Cook few minutes.

Cook chicken livers gently in 1 tablespoon butter 5 to 8 minutes, depending on their size. Chop livers roughly; divide between soup cups before pouring on hot soup. Sprinkle with chopped parsley. Makes 4 to 6 servings.

Turkey and Chestnut Soup

3 to 4 tablespoons or more of leftover chestnut stuffing (or 5 to 6 tablespoons canned chestnut puree)	5 to 6 cups water
	Salt and pepper
	1 tablespoon butter
Carcass of one cooked turkey	¾ tablespoon all-purpose flour
2 onions, sliced	
2 to 3 carrots, sliced	*Garnish*
2 to 3 stalks of celery, sliced	5 to 6 chestnuts
Several sprigs of parsley	1 tablespoon chopped parsley
1 bay leaf	

Remove remaining chestnut stuffing from cold turkey; reserve. Take off any pieces of turkey meat which can be used as a garnish. Break up turkey carcass; put into a large pan with sliced onions, carrots, celery, and herbs. Cover with water; simmer until well flavored. Avoid boiling hard; this makes stock cloudy. Strain.

Put chestnut stuffing into electric blender with a cup of turkey stock; blend until smooth. Turn into a pan; add remaining 4 cups stock, seasoning, and turkey meat. Cook together for a few minutes. If the soup is too thin, blend butter and flour together to make a paste; add to the soup in small pieces; stir until thickened. Bring to a boil; serve hot with a few cooked chestnuts, fried in butter, broken into pieces, and sprinkled on top with chopped parsley. Makes 4 to 6 servings.

Avocado Soup

Brown Bean Soup

Oxtail Soup

1	(2-pound) disjointed oxtail or 2 veal tails	½	cup carrots, diced
1	medium-sized onion, sliced	1	cup celery, diced
		1	bay leaf
2	tablespoons vegetable oil	½	cup tomatoes, drained
8	cups water	1	teaspoon dried thyme
1	teaspoon salt	1	tablespoon flour
4	peppercorns	1	tablespoon butter or margarine
¼	cup parsley, chopped	¼	cup Madeira

In 4-quart Dutch oven, brown oxtail and onion in hot oil several minutes. Add water, salt, and peppercorns; simmer uncovered about 2 hours. Cover; continue to simmer 3 additional hours. Add parsley, carrots, celery, bay leaf, tomatoes, and thyme; continue simmering, covered, 30 minutes longer or until vegetables are tender.

Strain stock and refrigerate an hour or more. In a blender, puree edible meat and vegetables; reserve. Remove fat from top of stock; reheat.

In a large, dry frying pan, brown flour over high heat. Cool slightly. Add butter or margarine; blend. A little at a time, add stock and vegetables. Correct seasoning; add Madeira just before serving. Makes 6 servings.

Seafood Soups

Maryland Crab Soup

6 cups strong Beef Stock (see Index)

3 cups mixed vegetables, fresh, leftover or frozen (include chopped onions and celery, diced carrots, peas, lima beans, cut string beans, corn, okra, and tomatoes; not squash, cabbage, or potatoes)

Seafood seasoning to taste

1 pound crab meat (claw or white meat)

Claws and pieces of whole crab if available (either raw or cooked)

Heat stock in a large soup pot. Add vegetables and seasoning; simmer 1 hour. Add crab meat and crab claws and pieces (if available) 30 minutes before serving. Simmer gently, to heat through and allow flavors to blend.

Serve hot in large soup bowls, with bread and butter or hard crusty rolls and butter as accompaniment. Makes 4 to 6 servings.

Creamy Crab Broccoli Soup

1	(6- to 8-ounce) package frozen Alaska king crab, thawed, or 1 (7½-ounce) can Alaska king crab	2	tablespoons flour
		2	cups milk
		2	cups half-and-half
		2	chicken bouillon cubes
1	(10-ounce) package frozen chopped broccoli	½	teaspoon salt
½	cup onion, chopped	⅛	teaspoon black pepper
3	tablespoons butter or margarine	⅛	teaspoon cayenne pepper
		¼	teaspoon thyme

Drain and slice crab. Cook broccoli according to package directions. Sauté onion in butter or margarine. Blend in flour. Add milk and half-and-half, stirring and cooking until thickened and smooth.

Dissolve bouillon cubes in hot soup. Add seasonings, crab, and broccoli; heat through. Makes 4 to 6 servings.

Cod Soup with Orange

⅔	pound cod fillets (frozen or fresh)	2	cloves garlic
			Salt
4	cups fish stock		Pepper
5 to 6	potatoes, cut into cubes		Juice from ½ orange or 2 to 3 tablespoons juice concentrate
1	whole fennel, cut into cubes		
1	leek, shredded	2	tablespoons snipped parsley
1	can crushed tomatoes		

Allow the fish to partially thaw, if frozen, and cut it into 1- to 1-1/2-inch wide cubes.

Bring the stock to a boil in a pot. Add vegetables and garlic. Season with salt and pepper, and let the soup simmer for 10 to 12 minutes until vegetables feel soft. Add orange juice and simmer soup for another 3 to 4 minutes. Serve soup piping hot with snipped parsley sprinkled on top. Makes 4 servings.

Cold Beet Soup with Sour Cream

Savory Shrimp Soup

1 medium-sized onion, chopped	1 (10-ounce) package frozen peas
1 large carrot, chopped	Salt and pepper to taste
1 tablespoon dry white wine	12 ounces medium cooked shrimp, canned or frozen
1 tablespoon water	
3 cups hot beef bouillon	½ cup white wine
1 teaspoon sage	¼ cup skim evaporated milk
1 teaspoon tarragon	

In 4-quart saucepan or Dutch oven, cook onion and carrot in 1 tablespoon wine and water until onion is soft. Add bouillon; simmer 12 minutes. Add sage, tarragon, and green peas. Bring to a boil; simmer 8 minutes.

Puree vegetable-bouillon mixture in a blender or food mill; return to pan. Season to taste with salt and pepper. Add shrimp; heat without boiling about 2 minutes. Stir in 1/2 cup white wine and the evaporated milk. Correct seasonings; serve immediately. Makes 4 servings.

Quick Bouillabaisse

1	onion	2	cups frozen peas
2	tablespoons margarine	1¼	pounds cod
½	teaspoon paprika	2	teaspoons salt
¾	quart fish stock	1	clove garlic
1	can tomatoes, chopped	⅓	cup mayonnaise

Juice of ½ lemon

Chop onion and fry until transparent in margarine in a large saucepan. Dust with paprika, then add fish stock. Bring to a boil and add tomatoes.

Squeeze in lemon juice and add peas, fish, and salt. Simmer for 5 minutes, or until fish portions are just cooked.

Meanwhile, crush garlic and add to mayonnaise. Serve the hot soup with a spoonful of the garlic mayonnaise and a hot, crusty bread. Makes 4 servings.

New England Clam Chowder

1	quart shucked clams, with liquid	1	bay leaf
3	slices salt pork, diced	1	cup water
2	small onions, minced	3	cups milk, scalded
2	medium-sized potatoes, diced	1½	cups half-and-half
		¼	cup butter
			Salt and freshly ground pepper

Drain clams, reserving liquor, then chop coarsely. Fry salt pork slowly in a kettle until all fat is rendered. Add onions; sauté until golden. Add potatoes, bay leaf, and water, then simmer until potatoes are tender.

Strain reserved clam liquor, then stir into potato mixture with milk, cream, butter, and chopped clams. Add seasonings, then simmer 15 minutes. Add more seasonings, if needed. Remove bay leaf before serving. Makes 6 to 8 servings.

Cauliflower Cream Soup

Neapolitan Fish Chowder

1	medium-sized onion, chopped	½	teaspoon salt
2	carrots, thinly sliced	1	(8-ounce) can tomato sauce
2	tablespoons parsley, minced	2	cups hot water
1	clove garlic, minced	1	small can whole baby clams (or minced clams)
2	tablespoons vegetable oil	1	pound fish fillets, cut in 1-inch pieces
¼	teaspoon pepper		

In a large frying pan, sauté onion, carrots, parsley, and garlic in hot oil until onion is soft. Add pepper, salt, tomato sauce, and 2 cups hot water. Bring to boil. Add clams with liquid and fish. Cover; simmer about 30 minutes. Makes 4 to 6 servings.

Vegetable Soups

Green Bean Soup

2 to 3 tablespoons butter
1   medium-sized onion (or 3 to 4 shallots), finely chopped
1   clove garlic, crushed
2   tablespoons flour
4   cups chicken or veal stock
Salt and pepper
1   pound green beans

1   teaspoon chopped or dried summer savory
A little green coloring if required

Garnish
4 to 6 tablespoons whipping cream
2 slices bacon

Melt butter; cook onion and garlic for 5 to 6 minutes in a covered pan. Add flour; blend in smoothly. Pour on stock and mix well. When smooth, bring to a boil, stirring constantly. Add salt and pepper.

String beans; cut in slanting slices or break in half depending on their size. Add to soup, with dried savory; cook for 25 minutes or until beans are tender.

Strain soup, reserving a few pieces of bean for garnish (keep warm). Put remaining soup and beans through a food mill or blend until smooth in electric blender. Reheat soup; adjust seasoning to taste; add a little green coloring if required.

Serve hot with a spoon of whipped cream on each cup; sprinkle with finely crumbled crispy fried bacon. Makes 4 to 6 servings.

Celery and Walnut Soup

Brown Bean Soup

⅔	pound brown beans/red kidney beans, dried	¼	teaspoon chili powder
6	cups water	4	cups vegetable broth (use the cooking water)
1	tablespoon salt	⅔	pound lean salted pork/ corned beef
1	large leek, peeled and finely chopped	1	tablespoon butter or margarine
1	green pepper, finely chopped	⅓	cup watercress, snipped
1	can tomatoes, strained		
1	clove garlic, crushed (optional)		

Place beans in a generous amount of water. Let stand overnight. Then pour off water.

Place beans in 6 cups water, add salt, and boil for 1-1/2 hours. Pour off water, but save it for the broth.

While beans are boiling, prepare and rinse vegetables. Stir all ingredients, except pork, butter, and watercress into bean stew. Boil soup over low heat for about 20 minutes. Stir soup vigorously so that beans break up. If you use a blender, the bean pieces will become too small.

Cut pork into strips and brown them in butter. Serve soup hot, garnished with the pork and watercress. Makes 4 servings.

Cold Asparagus Soup

1 can condensed asparagus soup	A little lemon juice
1 can green asparagus tips	A few drops of Tabasco
Milk	¼ cup heavy cream
1 carton natural yogurt	Paprika

Blend condensed asparagus soup with liquid from can of asparagus tips, using enough milk to fill soup can. Stir in yogurt, or blend in an electric blender. Add a little lemon juice and a few drops of Tabasco.

Stir in asparagus tips; serve chilled with a spoonful of whipped cream in each cup. Sprinkle with paprika. Makes 4 servings.

Lentil Soup

Avocado Soup

2 ripe, soft avocados, pitted and peeled	**1** cup light cream
1 teaspoon lemon juice	**½** cup plain yogurt
1 cup cold chicken broth	**½** cup dry white wine
	Salt to taste

Set aside a few thin slices of avocado brushed with lemon juice to use as a garnish. Place remaining avocado in a food processor or blender; blend until smooth. Add remaining ingredients· blend until smooth.

Serve soup very cold, garnished with reserved avocado slices. Makes 4 servings.

Cold Beet Soup with Sour Cream

2 (1-pound) cans diced beets, drained	¼ teaspoon white pepper
3 cups Beef Stock (see Index)	2 teaspoons celery salt
	¼ cup orange juice
1 teaspoon wine vinegar	1 carton sour cream
¼ cup Burgundy wine	1 tablespoon parsley, finely minced
1 tablespoon onion juice	

Combine half of the beets and a small amount of stock in a blender container; process until beets are pureed. Repeat the process, using remaining beets and a small amount of stock. Combine pureed beets mixture, remaining stock, vinegar, Burgundy, onion juice, seasonings, and orange juice; chill several hours.

Serve in individual soup bowls with a dollop of sour cream, sprinkled with parsley. Two pounds of fresh, cooked beets may be substituted for canned beets. Makes 8 to 10 servings.

Cauliflower Cream Soup

1 medium-sized cauliflower	1 tablespoon parsley, minced
1 medium-sized potato	½ teaspoon savory
1 large tomato	2 teaspoons salt
4 cups milk	¼ teaspoon white pepper
4 green onions or scallions, minced	1 cup whipping cream

Separate cauliflower into florets. Peel and dice potato; skin and chop tomato. Combine milk, cauliflower, potato, tomato, green onions, parsley, and seasonings in a heavy kettle. Simmer until the vegetables are tender. Pour soup through a colander, draining off liquid. Reserve liquid.

Place 1/3 of vegetables in the blender container with enough of liquid to blend easily; process until pureed. Repeat process with remaining vegetables.

Return puree and remaining liquid to kettle; stir in cream gradually. Place over low heat; heat through, stirring frequently. You may serve with a bowl of grated Parmesan cheese to sprinkle over the top. Makes 6 servings.

Soup with Red and Green Lentils

Cream of Broccoli Soup

8	cups water	1	teaspoon salt
3	cubes chicken bouillon	½	teaspoon pepper
2	(10-ounce) packages frozen broccoli, chopped	¾	cup powdered milk
2	tablespoons onion flakes	1	tablespoon sherry

In a saucepan, combine water and bouillon cubes. Bring to a boil. Add frozen broccoli, onion flakes, and seasonings. Bring to a boil, then reduce heat. Simmer for 15 minutes or until broccoli is tender. Cool slightly.

Put a third of the broccoli mixture into blender with 1/4 cup of the powdered milk. Blend until smooth. Pour into clean pan. Repeat until all broccoli and powdered milk is blended. Just before serving, heat, stirring in sherry. Makes 6 to 8 servings.

Cabbage Soup

1	small green cabbage (or 2 cups of shredded green cabbage)	2	tablespoons parsley, chopped
2	slices fat bacon	1	bay leaf
1	large onion, chopped		Salt and pepper
2	small leeks, white part only, sliced		A pinch of nutmeg
2	carrots, sliced	2	teaspoons chopped dill or 1 teaspoon dillseeds
1	potato, sliced		
1	tablespoon flour		*Garnish*
4	cups Brown Stock (see Index), or water and bouillon cubes; ham stock can be used, if not too salty		Fat for frying
		3 to 4	frankfurters

Slice and wash green cabbage; put into a pan of boiling salted water; cook 5 minutes. Drain and rinse under cold water.

Meanwhile, chop bacon; heat over gentle heat until fat runs. Add onion, leeks, carrots, and potato; stir over heat a few minutes. Sprinkle in flour; blend well before adding stock (or water and cubes). Add parsley, bay leaf, salt, and pepper. Bring to a boil. Reduce heat; simmer 10 minutes before adding cabbage. Cook 20 minutes more, or until vegetables are tender but not mushy.

Adjust seasoning; add nutmeg and chopped dill, or a few dillseeds. Remove bay leaf. For garnish, fry frankfurters and cut in slices, putting a few slices into each serving. Makes 4 to 6 servings.

Onion Soup

Carrot Soup

3 cups Chicken Stock (see Index)	2 tablespoons peanut butter
1 small onion, chopped	1 tablespoon Worcestershire sauce
4 carrots, peeled and sliced	1 clove garlic, minced
1/8 teaspoon nutmeg	Dash of Tabasco sauce

Simmer all ingredients together until tender, about 15 minutes. Remove half of carrots. Puree rest of ingredients.

Add reserved carrots; reheat before serving. Garnish with chopped peanuts, apples, and green onions. Makes 4 servings.

Celery and Walnut Soup

2 cups fresh celery sticks, cut in slices	⅓ cup heavy cream
1 medium-sized onion, chopped	⅓ cup walnut meats
3½ tablespoons butter	1½ tablespoons butter
4 cups chicken broth	Celery salt
	Freshly ground pepper
	A small amount of sherry

Combine sliced celery and onion. Place mixture in a frying pan with butter and allow to bubble slowly over low heat. Stir occasionally. Simmer for about 10 minutes, or until celery feels soft. Stir in 3-1/4 cups of the chicken broth. Bring to a boil and simmer for about 30 minutes.

Strain or mix in a food processor and pour soup back into pot. Beat in heavy cream. Chop walnut meats and fry them in butter for a few minutes; then blend them into the soup. Add celery salt, pepper, and sherry. Dilute with the rest of the chicken broth if soup feels too thick.

Serve in a heated soup bowl or in warmed individual serving bowls. Decorate with a few small leaves from the celery, which "swim" on the top of the soup. Makes 4 servings.

Cream of Corn Soup

3 tablespoons butter	1 chicken stock cube
1 onion, chopped	
1 medium-sized potato, finely sliced	*Garnish*
1½ cups fresh or canned corn	4 to 6 spoons heavy cream
3½ cups milk	1 tablespoon chopped chives or parsley (or a sprinkling of paprika)
1 bay leaf	
3 to 4 sprigs of parsley	Fried Bread Croutons (see Index)
Salt and pepper	
¼ teaspoon mace	

Melt butter; cook onion and potato gently with lid on pan 5 minutes, shaking pan occasionally to prevent sticking. Add 1 cup corn. Stir well. Add milk, bay leaf, parsley, salt, pepper, and mace. Bring to simmering heat; add a chicken stock cube; cook until vegetables are tender.

Put soup into electric blender; blend until smooth; or put through fine food mill. Return soup to pan with remaining corn (which if fresh should be simmered until tender in salted water). Reheat soup until nearly boiling; adjust seasoning.

Serve in soup cups with a spoonful of cream in each cup, a sprinkling of chopped chives, parsley or paprika, and Fried Bread Croutons. Makes 4 to 6 servings.

Pea Soup with Ham

Green Potato Soup

Old-Fashioned Corn Chowder

1	cup bacon, cubed	2	cups water
1	medium onion, diced	2	cups milk
4	tablespoons flour	1	teaspoon salt
2	cups raw potatoes, cubed	½	teaspoon pepper
2	cups corn, fresh, canned, or frozen		

Sauté bacon until crisp. Remove from pan. Fry onions in bacon fat until soft. Stir in flour. Add milk slowly, stirring until thick. Cook potatoes and corn in water until potatoes are tender. Add onion gravy to potato mixture. Add bacon and seasoning. Serve hot. Stir over flame until well mixed and mixture boils. Makes 6 to 8 servings.

Chilled Cucumber Soup

¼ cup shelled walnuts	⅓ cup cold water
1 large clove garlic, peeled	1 cucumber, peeled and chopped
3 tablespoons olive oil	
1 tablespoon white wine vinegar	Salt and pepper
	Chopped fresh mint or parsley
3 cups yogurt	

Combine walnuts, garlic, oil, and vinegar in a blender container; blend at medium speed until smooth. Mixture may also be mashed together with a mortar and pestle.

Combine yogurt and water in a mixing bowl; add walnut mixture. Stir until all ingredients are well mixed. Add cucumber and salt and pepper to taste. Chill several hours before serving. Garnish with fresh chopped mint or parsley. Makes 4 servings.

Lentil Soup

2 cups lentils	1 teaspoon salt
8 cups water	½ teaspoon pepper
½ cup onion, chopped	3 tablespoons tomato paste
2 cloves garlic, minced	2 bay leaves
½ cup carrots, chopped	½ teaspoon oregano
½ cup celery, chopped	3 tablespoons wine vinegar
¼ cup olive oil	

Wash and pick over lentils. Soak them overnight in 2 cups of water. In a Dutch oven or soup kettle, sauté onion, garlic, carrot, and celery in olive oil. Add lentils, 6 cups of water, salt, pepper, tomato paste, bay leaves, and oregano. Bring to a boil; cook 2-1/2 to 3 hours or until lentils are soft. Remove bay leaves.

At this point, mixture may be pureed in blender until smooth. Thin with water if necessary. Return mixture to soup pot; heat. Add wine vinegar; serve. Makes 6 to 8 servings.

Soup with Red and Green Lentils

1   large onion
2 to 3 cloves garlic
1   tablespoon butter
⅓   cup red lentils
⅓   cup green lentils or the same amount of white beans

6   cups meat broth
Sour cream

Chop onion into large pieces and crush garlic cloves. Melt butter in large pot and brown onion and garlic.

Stir in lentils and broth. Let soup simmer over low heat for 20 to 30 minutes, or until lentils feel soft. Serve with a dab of sour cream in the soup. Makes 4 servings.

Fresh Mushroom Soup

1   pound fresh mushrooms
2   tablespoons vegetable oil
2   scallions or shallots, minced
4   cups chicken broth or bouillon

¼   teaspoon salt
½   teaspoon lemon juice
1   lemon, sliced

Wash mushrooms; pat dry with paper towels. Chop very fine or chop small amounts at a time in blender on slowest speed.

Heat oil in frypan and sauté scallions about 3 minutes or until wilted. Add mushrooms; cook, stirring occasionally, about 5 minutes. Add broth, salt, and lemon juice. Bring to a boil. Reduce heat to a simmer and cook uncovered 30 minutes.

Blend finished soup in blender or press through a coarse sieve. If sieved, press hard on mushrooms to extract all liquid. Reheat before serving. Garnish with lemon slices. Makes 6 servings.

Cream of Mushroom Soup

¼   cup butter
½   cup onion, finely chopped
1   pound mushrooms
6   tablespoons flour
6   cups chicken broth
1   bay leaf
2   sprigs parsley
½   teaspoon salt

⅛   teaspoon pepper
2   tablespoons butter
1   tablespoon lemon juice
1   cup heavy cream or half-and-half
2   egg yolks
½   cup sour cream
Chopped parsley, if desired

Clear Tomato Soup

Melt butter in 3-quart saucepan. Add onion and stems from mushrooms; cook until onion is tender. Stir in flour, add broth. Cook over medium heat, stirring constantly, until thickened. Add bay leaf, parsley sprigs, salt, and pepper. Simmer 20 minutes. Strain; return to pan.

In small frying pan, sauté sliced mushroom caps in 2 tablespoons butter and lemon juice. Add to strained broth; simmer 10 minutes.

Blend cream and egg yolks. Slowly add small amount of soup to yolks, then add yolks to soup, stirring constantly. Heat gently 2 minutes. Stir in sour cream. Serve soup hot. Garnish with chopped parsley. Makes 8 servings.

Onion Soup

4	large onions, thinly sliced	Salt and pepper to taste	
1	tablespoon butter	4	slices French bread, cut ½ inch thick
1	tablespoon vegetable oil		
¼	teaspoon sugar	2	teaspoons vegetable oil
2	tablespoons flour	1	clove garlic, peeled and cut
6	cups beef broth	2	tablespoons cognac
¼	cup dry white wine or vermouth	1	cup Swiss cheese, grated

In covered 4-quart saucepan or Dutch oven, cook onions slowly with butter and 1 tablespoon oil for 15 minutes. Stir occasionally. Uncover; increase heat to moderate. Add sugar; sauté onions, stirring frequently, about 30 minutes or until onions turn golden brown. Sprinkle onions with flour; stir over heat 2 to 3 minutes. Blend in hot broth and wine; adjust seasonings. Simmer, partially covered, 1 hour.

Meanwhile, place bread slices in 350°F oven 30 minutes or until lightly toasted. Halfway through baking, baste each slice with 1/2 teaspoon oil; rub with cut garlic clove.

Before serving, add cognac; divide soup into ovenproof bowls or casseroles. Sprinkle 1/2 cup cheese in soup. Float slices of French bread on top of soup; sprinkle with rest of cheese.

Bake in preheated 325°F oven 15 to 20 minutes, until hot, then set under broiler 2 to 3 minutes, until cheese is golden brown. Serve immediately. Makes 4 servings.

Pea Soup with Ham

3	medium-sized onions	1	teaspoon marjoram
3	whole cloves	1	teaspoon thyme
1	pound yellow peas	Salt to taste	
4	cups water	Parsley for garnish	
1	pound ham		

Dice 2 onions. Peel third onion, but leave it whole. Stick cloves into whole onion. Put diced onions, whole onion, peas, and water into a pot. Cook them 20 minutes; add ham. Add marjoram and thyme; let it cook at least 1-1/2 hours. Remove cloved onion and ham. Cut ham into thick slices. Season soup with salt to taste.

When ready to serve, place a slice of ham on top of each serving of soup; garnish with parsley. Makes 4 to 6 servings.

Zorn Soup

Peanut Soup

2 tablespoons butter or margarine	½ cup cream-style peanut butter
5 green onions including tops, trimmed and sliced	1½ teaspoons lemon juice
1 celery stalk, minced	⅛ teaspoon liquid red pepper seasoning (optional)
3 tablespoons flour	¼ cup chopped roasted peanuts for garnish
1 (10¾-ounce) can chicken broth	2 tablespoons minced chives for garnish
2 cups milk	

Sauté green onions and celery in melted butter for 12 to 15 minutes or until tender. Blend in flour. Slowly add chicken broth and milk, stirring constantly until thickened.

Strain soup. Puree onions and celery in blender. Combine puree with soup in kettle and reheat. Beat in peanut butter. Add lemon juice and seasonings. Heat, stirring occasionally, for 15 to 20 minutes. Do not boil.

Top individual servings with chopped peanuts and minced chives. Makes 6 servings.

Potato Soup

2 tablespoons margarine	Salt and pepper
2 tablespoons onion, finely chopped	1 cup milk
1 cup potato, diced	1 tablespoon parsley, chopped
4 tablespoons water	A pinch of nutmeg
½ clove garlic, crushed	

Heat margarine in a pan; add onion and potato; sauté about 5 minutes. Add water, garlic, and a little salt and pepper. Cover; cook over low heat until potato is quite soft.

Add milk; stir until soup boils. Then mash through a sieve. Return to pan; adjust seasoning. Add parsley and a pinch of nutmeg; reheat before serving. Makes 3 to 4 servings.

Green Potato Soup

4 to 5 potatoes	1 teaspoon salt
1 onion	Black pepper
4 cups chicken broth	1 (10-ounce) package frozen chopped kale

Peel potatoes and onion; cut them into pieces. Bring broth to a boil. Add potatoes and onion. Cover and boil for about 25 minutes, or until potatoes become mushy.

Add kale. When it is tender, beat mixture with a whisk so that potatoes get mashed. Season and serve. Makes 4 servings.

Bacon and Cheese Appetizers

Sherry Bisque

1	small ham hock	3	tablespoons flour
¾	cup split green peas	1	(8-ounce) can tomato
1	bay leaf		puree
6	cups beef broth	1	cup chicken broth
6	slices bacon, diced	⅓	cup sherry
¾	cup onion, chopped	¼	cup butter
1	stalk celery, diced		Freshly ground pepper to taste

Place ham hock, split peas, bay leaf, and 4 cups beef broth into 4-quart saucepan. Bring to a boil; reduce heat and simmer. Sauté bacon in frying pan until fat is rendered. Add onion and celery; cook until tender. Stir in flour; mix to blend. Add remaining 2 cups beef broth; cook until slightly thickened. Add onion mixture to split-pea mixture; continue to cook until split peas are soft, about 1-1/2 hours.

When done, remove ham hock. Puree mixture in blender or food mill. Add tomato puree, chicken broth, and sherry. Add butter and pepper; stir until melted. Strain soup, if desired, before serving. Makes 8 to 12 servings.

Spinach Soup

2	pounds fresh spinach or 2 packages frozen chopped spinach	2	tablespoons flour
		1	teaspoon salt
2	quarts Chicken Stock (see Index)		Dash of freshly ground pepper
		⅛	teaspoon nutmeg
3	tablespoons butter		Hard-cooked egg for garnish (optional)

Thoroughly wash spinach, then drain it. Chop it coarsely. If frozen spinach is used, thaw it completely and drain it. Bring soup stock to a boil in a 4-quart pot; add spinach. Simmer it uncovered about 8 minutes. Strain spinach from stock into separate bowls. Press spinach with a spoon to remove most liquid. If desired, chop cooked spinach even finer.

Melt butter in soup pot, then remove it from heat. Stir in flour, being careful to avoid lumps. Add liquid stock, 1 cup at a time, stirring constantly. Return it to heat; bring it to a boil. Add spinach, salt, pepper, and nutmeg. The soup will thicken slightly. Simmer about 5 minutes more.

Serve soup, garnishing each serving with a few slices of hard-cooked egg, if desired. Makes 4 to 6 servings.

Cheese Mold

Clear Tomato Soup

1	pound very ripe tomatoes	1	teaspoon dried basil
3	pints Chicken Stock (see Index)	1	teaspoon salt
		⅛	teaspoon white pepper

Cut tomatoes in large chunks; place in small saucepan. Add 1/2 cup stock and basil. Simmer 20 minutes. Force tomato mixture through a sieve into a bowl. Let set for several minutes.

Pour remaining stock in a medium saucepan; add tomato mixture except sediment in bottom of bowl. Add salt and pepper. Simmer until soup is reduced to about 2 pints. Float a basil leaf on top if available. Makes 4 to 6 servings.

Spring Soup

4 young carrots
2 to 3 young leeks, according to size (or 8 to 10 scallions)
3 tablespoons butter
1½ tablespoons flour
4 cups Chicken Stock (see Index) or water and chicken cubes
½ cup cauliflower florets
2 to 3 tablespoons peas

2 to 3 tablespoons young green beans, sliced
A little sugar
2 tablespoons mixed parsley, chervil, mint, and thyme
Salt and pepper

Liaison ·
½ cup cream
2 egg yolks

Peel and dice carrots. Wash leeks or scallions thoroughly; cut white part into slices. Melt butter; cook these vegetables gently in a covered pan 5 to 6 minutes without allowing to brown. Sprinkle in flour, mix thoroughly, then add stock. Blend well until smooth; bring to a boil, stirring constantly. Cook a few minutes before adding cauliflower florets, peas, sliced beans, and sugar. Simmer 15 minutes. Add herbs; cook a few more minutes, to draw out flavor of herbs. Season to taste.

Make liaison by mixing cream with egg yolks. Take a few spoonfuls of hot soup; mix well with cream and egg-yolk mixture before straining it back into soup, stirring constantly. Reheat, being very careful not to allow soup to boil, as this causes egg to curdle and spoils texture of soup. Makes 4 to 6 servings.

Winter Squash Soup

1 medium-sized winter squash, peeled and chopped
½ medium-sized onion, chopped
1 handful celery leaves, chopped
1 medium-sized tomato, chopped

8 cups water or more
Salt and pepper to taste
2 tablespoons brown sugar
1 teaspoon cinnamon
Drippings from steak and onions for seasoning

Cover squash with water in large soup kettle. Add chopped onion, celery leaves, and tomato. Bring to a boil. Reduce heat and simmer until squash is tender. Season with salt and pepper to taste.

Add brown sugar and cinnamon. Serve with drippings from steak and onions to season. Makes 4 servings.

Cold Tomato and Vegetable Soup

8 large tomatoes, peeled and seeded	**3** cloves garlic, peeled
2 medium-sized cucumbers, peeled and seeded	**⅓** cup olive oil
2 large green peppers, seeds and pith removed	**1** cup rich beef bouillon
1 cup sweet onion, finely chopped	**½** tablespoon lemon juice
	Salt and freshly ground black pepper

Finely chop about 2/3 of tomatoes. Set aside in large bowl. Finely chop cucumbers, peppers, and onion, adding each vegetable with its juices to large bowl.

Puree remaining tomatoes, garlic, and olive oil; pour over chopped vegetables along with bouillon and lemon juice. Add salt and pepper to taste. Refrigerate several hours. Before serving, sample; adjust seasonings; add a little bouillon to thin soup, if needed. Makes 6 servings.

Party Croissant

New England Vegetable Chowder

¼ cup butter or margarine	½ teaspoon salt
1 small onion, chopped	⅛ teaspoon pepper
1 green pepper, chopped	2 tablespoons parsley,
1 cup celery, diced	chopped
1 cup carrots, diced	4 cups milk
1½ cups whole kernel corn	Grated American cheese for
1 cup cabbage, grated	garnish
1 cup peas	

Melt butter in heavy kettle. Add onion, green pepper, and celery. Sauté until limp. Add rest of the vegetables and seasoning. Add enough water to cover. Cook 1 hour.

Stir in milk and parsley. Ladle into soup bowls. Sprinkle with cheese. Makes 4 to 6 servings.

Watercress Soup

2 bunches fresh watercress	2 cups milk
3 tablespoons butter	¼ teaspoon mace
1 potato, sliced	A little green coloring
1 small onion, finely	(optional)
chopped	
1 tablespoon flour	*Garnish*
3 cups White or Chicken	4 to 6 tablespoons cream
Stock (see Index), or water	Watercress sprigs
3 to 4 sprigs of parsley	Fried Bread Croutons (see
1 bay leaf	Index)
Salt and pepper	

Wash and pick over watercress, discarding any yellow leaves. Reserve enough green top-sprigs to make final garnish; chop remaining cress roughly. Melt butter; cook potato and onion together 2 to 3 minutes before adding chopped watercress. Continue cooking 3 to 4 minutes, stirring constantly to prevent browning. Sprinkle in flour; blend well. Add stock; blend together before bringing to a boil. Add herbs and some seasoning; reduce heat. Simmer until potato is tender, about 20 minutes.

Remove bay leaf. Put soup into electric blender; blend until smooth, or put through fine food mill or sieve. Return soup to pan; reheat gently. At same time, heat milk in a separate pan. When almost at boiling point, pour into watercress mixture (this makes texture of soup lighter and more delicate). Adjust seasoning, adding mace and a little green coloring if desired.

Serve with a spoon of cream in each cup and reserved watercress sprigs on top. Fried Bread Croutons are also excellent with this soup. Makes 4 to 6 servings.

Yarmouth Straws

Zorn Soup

¾ **cup dried green peas**	2¾ **to 3 pounds beef, for**
12 **cups of water**	**example shoulder roast**
3 **tablespoons salt**	8 **potatoes**
3 **onions, peeled and cut**	4 **carrots**
into wedges	1 **wedge cabbage, about ½**
10 **black peppercorns**	**pound**
2 **bay leaves**	**Snipped parsley**

Soak peas in 4 cups of the water and 1 tablespoon of the salt for 8 to 10 hours. Pour away the water. Place peas in a pot with the remaining 8 cups of water. Cook peas together with the onions and spices for about 45 minutes. Skim away all the pea skins.

Rinse meat under running water. Stick a meat thermometer into the beef so that the point of the thermometer comes to the middle of the thickest part of the meat. The entire stick of the thermometer should be in the meat. Place meat in the pot. Boil over low heat for 1-1/4 to 1-1/2 hours, until thermometer shows 185 to 195°F.

Peel potatoes and carrots about 30 minutes before meat is done. Cut vegetables into chunks and cook them in the soup. Add shredded cabbage about 10 minutes before meat is done. Season to taste.

When meat is done, remove pot from the stove. Let it stand, covered, for about 20 minutes. Remove meat from the soup, cut it into slices, and serve it on a plate with the soup. Or cut pieces of the meat into the soup. Garnish with parsley and serve. Makes 8 servings.

Cheese and Egg Appetizers

Cheese Crisps

½ **pound Cheddar cheese, grated (2 cups)**
⅓ **cup Parmesan cheese, grated**
½ **cup butter or margarine, room temperature**
¼ **cup water**
¾ **cup whole-wheat pastry flour**

⅓ **cup all-purpose flour**
1 **tablespoon wheat germ, toasted**
¼ **teaspoon salt**
Dash of cayenne (optional)
1 **cup rolled oats**
⅛ **teaspoon paprika**

Thoroughly blend cheeses, butter, and water. Add flours, wheat germ, salt, and cayenne; mix well. Stir in rolled oats.

Divide dough in half. Form into 2 rolls, each about 1-1/2 inches in diameter (about 6 inches long). Wrap tightly; refrigerate until well chilled, about 4 hours, or up to 1 week.

Slice 1/8 to 1/4 inch thick; sprinkle with paprika. Bake on greased baking sheet at 400°F 8 to 10 minutes. Cool on rack.

If less uniform shape is desired, dough can be shaped into small (1-1/4-inch) balls immediately after mixing; flatten with hands onto baking sheet. Sprinkle with paprika. Bake in 400°F oven 8 to 10 minutes, until golden brown. Makes 48 crisps.

Bacon and Cheese Appetizers

1	cup Cheddar cheese	2	tablespoons catsup
8	strips streaky bacon	16	cocktail sticks

Cut cheese into 16 pieces. Spread bacon strips on a board with a round-bladed knife and cut in half. Cover broiler pan with foil. Lay bacon on pan and broil until cooked but not browned, turning once.

Spread bacon with catsup, then wrap them around the pieces of cheese and secure with a wooden cocktail stick. Return to broiler until cheese begins to melt. Serve immediately. Makes 16 appetizers.

Cheddar-Cheese Puffs

2	cups Cheddar cheese, grated	½	teaspoon salt
½	cup butter or margarine, softened	½	teaspoon paprika
1	cup flour, sifted	48	small green olives, stuffed with pimientos

Blend cheese with butter. Add flour, salt, and paprika; mix well. Mold 1 teaspoon dough around each olive to cover. At this point you can refrigerate or freeze puffs for up to 10 days.

Bake puffs at 400°F for 15 minutes. Serve hot. Makes 48 puffs.

Fried-Cheese Profiteroles

⅓	cup all-purpose flour	¼	cup butter, softened
⅓	cup Parmesan cheese, freshly grated	2	eggs
			Paprika

Blend flour with cheese. Combine butter with 1/2 cup water in small saucepan. Bring to boil, stirring until butter melts. Add flour mixture all at once; stir vigorously with wooden spoon until mixture is smooth and leaves sides of pan, forming a ball. Remove from heat.

Add 1 egg; beat 1 minute, until well mixed. Repeat procedure with remaining egg; beat until smooth and thickened. Let stand, covered, at room temperature until completely cool. Do not refrigerate.

Spoon mixture into pastry bag with 1/2-inch tip affixed. Pipe 1/2-inch pieces or drop by teaspoonfuls into 350°F oil in deep-fat fryer. Fry until golden; drain well on absorbent toweling. Sprinkle with paprika. Makes 40 to 50 small puffs.

Cottage Orange Cups

Cheese Mold

6 ounces blue cheese	**Dash of cayenne**
¾ cup butter	**Ground pistachio nuts**

Soften cheese, cream until smooth. Cream butter until light and fluffy. Blend cheese, butter, and cayenne together.

Line small mold with 3 layers cheesecloth, overlapping at top. Press cheese into mold. Cover top of cheese with overlapping cheesecloth. Refrigerate 24 hours.

Lift cheese out of mold, using cheesecloth. Turn onto serving dish. Carefully remove cheesecloth. Smooth rough edges with damp metal spatula. Sprinkle with pistachio nuts. Makes 1-1/2 cups.

Greek Spinach and Cheese Turnovers

1 **egg**	1 **tablespoon parsley, chopped**
½ **medium-sized onion, finely chopped**	½ **teaspoon dillweed**
¼ **pound feta cheese, crumbled**	½ **teaspoon garlic powder**
4 **ounces cream cheese**	6 **sheets phyllo or 4 frozen patty shells (omit butter when using patty shells)**
5 **ounces (½ of 10-ounce package) frozen chopped spinach, thawed and drained**	1 **stick butter, melted**

In blender or mixer bowl combine egg, onion, and feta cheese; beat to combine. Add cream cheese; combine well. Add spinach and seasonings; mix just until blended. Chill 1 hour.

If made with phyllo dough: Phyllo must be handled with great care, since it is very delicate and dry to the touch. Carefully unroll as many sheets as needed; store remainder immediately.

Place the sheets not immediately in use between linen tea towels to prevent drying. If weather is very hot and dry, sprinkle a little water on towels.

Phyllo sheets are generally 16 × 22 inches. Stack 2 leaves together, cutting through both sheets. Cut strips 2 inches wide by 16 inches long. Brush with melted butter. Place a teaspoon of filling on 1 end of strip. Fold 1 corner of strip to opposite side, forming a triangle and enclosing filling. Continue folding as you would an American flag, to end of strip, maintaining triangular shape. Brush with melted butter.

Place on ungreased cookie sheet. Bake at 375°F 20 minutes. Serve hot.

If made with puff pastry dough: Defrost patty shells at room temperature 15 to 20 minutes. Form each shell into a ball; roll on floured pastry cloth to 11 × 11-inch square. Cut into 16 individual squares. Place 1/2 teaspoon filling on each square. Fold to form a triangle; seal with milk.

Bake at 450°F 12 minutes. Makes about 33 if made with phyllo; about 64 if made with puff pastry.

Note: These can be baked, then frozen. Reheat on cookie sheet at 350°F 15 minutes.

Stuffed Eggs

Stuffed Eggs

4	eggs	Salt and pepper	
½	level teaspoon dried parsley or ½ level tablespoon fresh parsley	4	level tablespoons mayonnaise

Hard-boil eggs in boiling water to cover for 10 to 15 minutes. Stir cooking eggs for the first 2 minutes to help keep yolks in the middle. Drain and cool eggs in cold water.

Shell and cut each egg in half lengthwise. Scoop out yolks into a bowl; add parsley, salt and pepper, and mayonnaise. Beat until smooth. Pile yolks back into whites or pipe them with a large star pipe. Makes 4 servings.

Party Croissant

1 ounce yeast	**Filling**
5 tablespoons butter or margarine	5 ounces garlic cheese
⅔ cup lukewarm water	¼ pound smoked ham, in thin slices
Salt	18 to 20 pimiento-filled olives
½ teaspoon sugar	
2 eggs	
1 tablespoon sesame seeds, without skins, plus more to sprinkle over croissant	
2 cups flour	

Crumble yeast in a large bowl. Melt butter in a pot and add water. Pour a little of the warm liquid over yeast and stir. Pour in rest of liquid. Add salt, sugar, 1 egg, and sesame seeds. Add nearly all of the flour and work until dough becomes smooth and shiny. Let rise under a cloth for about 30 minutes.

Place dough onto a lightly floured baking board and knead it until it stops sticking to the board. Roll out dough into a triangle. Lay filling in an even strip across the widest part of the triangle. Roll together toward the point. Form into a croissant.

Place croissant on a prepared baking sheet and let it rise for approximately 20 minutes. Brush with second egg and sprinkle some sesame seeds over croissant. Bake at 400°F on lowest rack in the oven for about 20 minutes. Test with a toothpick. Makes 8 servings.

Yarmouth Straws

Pastry:	Cold water to mix
1 cup flour	
Salt and pepper	**Filling**
6 tablespoons margarine	2 kipper fillets
⅓ cup cheese, grated	1 egg yolk
1 egg yolk	Milk for brushing

Make pastry. Sift flour with a little salt and pepper into a bowl. Add margarine and rub it in with your fingertips until mixture resembles fine bread crumbs. Stir in cheese, egg yolk, and enough cold water to form a firm dough. Knead lightly on a lightly floured surface and roll out to a 10-inch square. Cut in half to make 2 strips.

Make the filling: Cook the kipper fillets by poaching in water or grilling. Remove any skin and bones, then flake the kippers into a bowl. Add the egg yolk and beat well together to a smooth paste. Brush a little milk around the edges of the strips of pastry. Spread the filling on one strip,

Onion Party Dip

cover with the other, and press down well all around. Cut into straws not more than 1/2 inch wide. Place on a baking tray and bake in a 400°F oven for 10 to 15 minutes or until crisp and golden brown. Makes 16 cheese straws.

Cottage Orange Cups

4	small oranges	1	level teaspoon confectioners' sugar
1	cup cottage cheese		Mint leaves for garnish
2	sticks celery, chopped		
1	dessert apple, peeled, cored, and chopped		

Slice tops off oranges about 1/3 of the way down. Carefully scoop out orange flesh with a spoon. Reserve skins. Put orange flesh and cottage cheese into an electric blender and blend at high speed until smooth. Alternatively, chop orange finely and beat it into cottage cheese; do not include the juice. Stir in celery, apple, and sugar.

Pile filling into reserved orange skins. Chill well before serving. Garnish with sprigs of mint. Makes 4 servings.

Meat and Chicken Appetizers

Chicken Pâté Cream

Bacon fat	½ **teaspoon freshly ground**
2 **tablespoons butter**	**pepper**
1½ **pounds chicken livers**	3 **green onions or shallots,**
½ **pound unsalted pork fat,**	**chopped**
ground	1 **clove garlic, minced**
2 **tablespoons dry sherry**	1½ **teaspoons salt**
2 **tablespoons brandy**	

Coat 7-inch soufflé mold well with cold bacon fat.

Melt butter in skillet. Sauté livers until all pink has disappeared. Combine livers, pork fat, sherry, brandy, pepper, onions, garlic, and salt; mix well. Place mixture in blender or food-processor container, a small amount at a time; blend until thoroughly pureed. Blending may take longer than usual; pork fat is not easily pureed. Spoon mixture into prepared mold; cover with aluminum foil. Place mold in baking dish. Pour hot water half the depth of mold.

Bake in preheated 350°F oven 1 hour. Remove from oven; let cool. Invert onto serving platter; chill in refrigerator overnight.

Serve with French bread or crackers. Makes about 2 cups.

Party Liver Pâté

¼ **pound butter or chicken fat**	1 **pound chicken livers**
1 **large onion, finely chopped**	1 **tablespoon Worcestershire sauce** **Salt and pepper to taste**

Melt butter in medium skillet; lightly brown chopped onion. Add chicken livers; cook until slightly pink at center, about 5 minutes. Remove from heat.

Put entire mixture through food mill until ground very smooth. If you use a colander instead of a food mill, you may want to put the liver mixture through twice to ensure a smooth texture. Add Worcestershire sauce and salt and pepper; mix together well with spoon.

Shape pâté into greased mold for a party. Turn out on serving plate; surround with party crackers so that guests can help themselves. Makes 10 to 16 servings.

Creamy Curry Dip

Swedish Meatballs

1	**pound ground beef**
¼	**pound ground veal**
¼	**pound ground pork**
2	**cups bread crumbs**
½	**cup milk**
1	**onion, diced fine**
2	**tablespoons butter**
2½	**teaspoons salt**
¼	**teaspoon pepper**
2	**teaspoons nutmeg**
2	**teaspoons paprika**
1	**teaspoon dry mustard**
3	**beaten eggs**
4	**tablespoons butter or margarine**

Sauce

¼	**teaspoon garlic, minced**
5	**tablespoons butter**
2	**teaspoons tomato paste**
1	**teaspoon beef concentrate**
2	**cups bouillon or soup stock**
1	**teaspoon aromatic bitters (optional)**
1	**cup sour cream**

This recipe improves if made one day ahead of time.

Have meat ground together twice. Soak bread crumbs in milk. Add meat; mix. Sauté onion in large skillet in 2 tablespoons butter. Mix together seasonings, eggs, onion, and meat in bowl. Mix well; form into 48 small balls.

Melt butter in skillet; brown meatballs on all sides. Remove; set aside to make sauce.

To make sauce, add garlic and 1 tablespoon butter to fat left in skillet. Sauté 1 minute. Blend in 4 more tablespoons butter, tomato paste, beef concentrate, and stock. Add bitters; stir mixture over low heat until it thickens. Pour sauce into lighted chafing dish. Stir in sour cream. Add meatballs to sauce, stirring once or twice to be sure all heats through.

Sauce can be poured into casserole dish and heated in oven, if preferred. Makes 48 meatballs.

Cocktail Meatballs

1	**pound lean hamburger**
1	**teaspoon garlic powder**
1	**(12-ounce) bottle chili sauce**
1	**(10-ounce) jar grape jelly**

Mix hamburger with garlic powder; shape into small balls. Pan-fry until well cooked; drain.

Mix chili sauce and jelly. Add meatballs; heat mixture. Serve warm in chafing dish with toothpicks nearby. Makes 12 servings.

Pickled Fish

Ham Appetizer

- 2 tablespoons green pepper, finely chopped
- 2 tablespoons celery, finely chopped
- 2 tablespoons pimiento, finely chopped
- ¼ teaspoon Dijon mustard
- 2 teaspoons lemon juice
- 2 teaspoons olive oil
- Salt and pepper
- 4 slices cooked ham
- Stuffed olives or gherkins for garnish

Mix green pepper, celery, and pimiento together. Mix mustard with lemon juice and oil. Add salt and pepper to taste. Pour over vegetables; mix well. Divide equally between ham slices. Fold over; secure with toothpicks.

Arrange on serving dish; garnish with stuffed olives or gherkins cut into fan shapes.

This can be served as a first course for a dinner party, or each roll can be cut into 4 portions, speared with toothpicks, and served on a canapé tray. Makes 4 servings.

Oriental Cocktail Kebabs

1 (15¼-ounce) can
pineapple chunks, drained
1 (1-pound) package brown-
and-serve sausages, cooked
according to package
directions, cut into thirds
1 (8-ounce) can water
chestnuts, halved
2 green peppers, cut into ¾-
inch squares

¼ pound small mushrooms,
stemmed
Reserved syrup from drained
pineapple
4 tablespoons soy sauce
3 slices fresh gingerroot
3 tablespoons brown sugar
2 tablespoons dry sherry

Alternate pieces of pineapple, sausage, water chestnuts, green pepper, and mushrooms on toothpicks.

Combine remaining ingredients; heat in skillet. Add kebabs. Cover; simmer 10 minutes. Remove from skillet. Stand the kebabs up in a wire-mesh trivet, leaving the exposed toothpicks dry. Makes 40 to 50 kebabs.

Pigs in Blankets

6 frankfurters
Prepared mustard
6 thin fingers cheese

Flaky Pastry
Egg or milk to glaze

Split frankfurters. Spread very lightly with mustard; insert a finger of cheese in each.

Roll pastry thin; cut into 6-inch squares. Place 1 frankfurter diagonally on each square; bring together other two diagonal corners of pastry so that ends of frankfurters are exposed.

Put onto baking sheet; glaze with egg or milk. Bake 20 minutes in a preheated 450°F oven.

Cut into small pieces and spear with toothpicks. Serve hot, with or without a mustard sauce. Makes 6 servings.

Mousse with Smoked Herring

Nuts and Dips

Salted Almonds

2 cups shelled almonds	Salt to taste
¼ cup salad oil	

Pour almonds into boiling water in large saucepan. Remove from heat; let stand about 5 minutes or until skins are soft. Drain; remove skins. Spread almonds on cookie pan; let stand until dry. Sprinkle with oil; stir until almonds are coated evenly. Sprinkle with salt; stir again.

Bake in preheated 350°F oven until lightly browned, stirring frequently. Cool; store in airtight container. Makes 2 cups.

Curried Nuts

¼ cup olive oil	⅛ teaspoon cayenne
1 tablespoon curry powder	2 cups nuts (assorted are best)
1 tablespoon Worcestershire sauce	

Combine oil and seasonings in medium-sized skillet. When mixture is hot, add nuts; stir constantly until nuts are completely coated.

Line baking pan with brown paper. Spread out nuts. Bake at 300°F 10 minutes. Nuts should be crisp. Makes 2 cups.

Spiced Herring

Onion Party Dip

1	**package French onion soup**
1	**cup natural yogurt**
2	**cloves garlic, crushed**
1	**tablespoon milk**

Salt and pepper
1 teaspoon lemon juice
2 tablespoons chopped chives

Combine all ingredients in a bowl and stir well with a wooden spoon. Leave to stand for at least 3 hours before serving—this allows dip to thicken. Serve in a bowl or, as in the picture, in a small scooped-out whole Edam cheese. Makes 4 to 6 servings.

Avocado Dip

3	ripe avocados		Dash of ground coriander
1	tomato, peeled and seeded	1	tablespoon lemon juice
1	small red onion, finely diced	1	tablespoon vinegar
1	tablespoon hot jalapeno pepper, chopped	2	tablespoons salad oil
		1	teaspoon salt

Mince avocados and tomato. Stir in all other ingredients. Serve with raw vegetables or corn chips.

You can use scooped-out avocado shells for serving dishes if this is to be served at table. For cocktail parties use a pretty bowl.

If made ahead of time, put avocado seeds in mixture to keep it green. Makes 2 cups.

Creamy Curry Dip

1	tablespoon margarine	½	cup cottage cheese, sieved
1	onion, finely chopped	2	tablespoons lemon juice
1	level teaspoon curry powder	4	tablespoons milk
½	cup Cheddar cheese, grated		

Heat margarine in a frying pan. Add onion and fry until soft (about 5 minutes). Stir in curry powder, then put aside to cool. Stir grated cheese into cottage cheese with a tablespoon, then beat in lemon juice, milk, and cold onion mixture until all are thoroughly combined. Makes 8 servings.

Apple-Nut Horseradish Dip

2	apples, peeled and cored	2	tablespoons minced or ground walnuts
1	tablespoon lemon juice		
¼	cup yogurt		
1	tablespoon prepared horseradish		

Grate apples; immediately combine with lemon juice to prevent discoloration. Blend in remaining ingredients.

Serve dip at once with chips, crackers, or vegetable dippers. Makes about 1 cup.

Clamdigger Dip

1 (7½- or 8-ounce) can minced clams
1 (8-ounce) package cream cheese, softened
1 tablespoon lemon juice
1 tablespoon onion, grated
1 teaspoon parsley, chopped
1 teaspoon Worcestershire sauce
¼ teaspoon salt
⅛ teaspoon liquid hot pepper sauce
Assorted chips, crackers, or raw vegetables

Drain clams; reserve liquid. Cream the cheese. Add seasonings and clams; mix thoroughly. Chill at least 1 hour to blend flavors. If necessary to thin dip, add clam liquid gradually.

Serve with chips, crackers, or vegetables. Makes 1-1/3 cups.

Garden Dip

⅔ cup low-fat cottage cheese
1 tablespoon onion, finely grated
1 tablespoon carrot, finely grated
1 teaspoon green pepper, finely chopped
½ teaspoon salt
Dash of garlic salt
1 cup plain yogurt

In small bowl, mash cottage cheese with fork. Add onion, carrot, pepper, salt, and garlic salt; beat until fairly smooth. Stir in yogurt. Cover; chill several hours.

Serve as dip with chips or raw vegetables. Makes 1-3/4 cups.

Shrimp Dip

½ pound fresh or frozen shrimp, cooked and cleaned, or 1 (5-ounce) can
1 cup cream-style cottage cheese
3 tablespoons chili sauce
2 teaspoons lemon juice
½ teaspoon onion juice
¼ teaspoon Worcestershire sauce
About ⅓ cup milk

Finely chop shrimp. Combine shrimp, cheese, chili sauce, lemon juice, onion juice, and Worcestershire sauce; blend in blender. Gradually beat in enough milk to give good dipping consistency.

Serve with potato chips, crackers, or celery. Makes about 2 cups.

Seafood Appetizers

Stuffed Clams

2 **dozen clams (littleneck or rock)**	¼ **teaspoon pepper**
¾ **cup dry white wine**	½ **teaspoon allspice**
¼ **cup water**	¼ **teaspoon cinnamon**
½ **teaspoon salt**	3 **tablespoons currants**
3 **tablespoons olive oil**	3 **tablespoons pine nuts**
½ **cup onion, chopped**	2 **tablespoons parsley, chopped**
½ **cup raw long-grain rice**	

Scrub clams; soak in several changes of cold water to remove sand. Place in skillet with wine, water, and salt. Cover; steam until shells open. Discard any clams that do not open. Cool; remove clams from shells. Save shells; strain pan juices.

Heat oil in medium saucepan. Sauté onion until golden. Add rice and 1 cup juices; bring to boil. Cover; reduce heat to low. Cook 15 minutes. Add pepper, spices, currants, pine nuts, and parsley. Cook 5 minutes; cool. Dice clams and add to pilaf.

Stuff shells with rice mixture; chill. Makes 24 appetizers.

Crab Balls

1	pound crab meat
4	tablespoons butter or margarine
1	teaspoon salt
⅛	teaspoon cayenne pepper
1	teaspoon dry mustard
1	teaspoon dehydrated parsley flakes
2	teaspoons Worcestershire sauce
½	cup soft bread crumbs
2	egg yolks, lightly beaten
½	cup flour
	Oil for frying

Pick over crab meat; remove any bits of shell and cartilage. Flake crab meat; place in mixing bowl.

Melt butter in small saucepan. Add seasonings, bread crumbs, and egg yolks to crab; mix well. Refrigerate 2 to 3 hours or until stiff enough to be handled easily. Form into 35 small balls the size of a walnut; dredge in flour.

Heat several inches of oil in heavy saucepan or deep-fat fryer to 360°F. Fry crab balls until golden brown; serve hot. Garnish with parsley and lemon wedges. Makes 35 crab balls.

Crab Dabs

1	(12-ounce) can dungeness or other crab meat, fresh or frozen, or 2 cans (6½ or 7½ ounces each) crab meat
⅓	cup fine soft bread crumbs
2	tablespoons dry sherry
1	teaspoon chopped chives
1	teaspoon dry mustard
¼	teaspoon salt
10	slices bacon, cut into thirds

Thaw crab meat, if frozen. Drain crab meat; remove any shell or cartilage. Chop crab meat.

Combine all ingredients except bacon; mix thoroughly. Chill 30 minutes. Divide crab mixture by tablespoons; shape into small rolls. Wrap bacon around crab rolls; secure with toothpicks. Place crab rolls on broiler pan. Broil about 4 inches from source of heat 8 to 10 minutes or until bacon is crisp. Turn carefully. Broil 4 to 5 minutes longer or until bacon is crisp. Makes about 30 hors d'oeuvres.

Oysters on the Half Shell

24 oysters	**Lemon wedges**
Beds of lettuce or crushed ice	**Tabasco sauce**

Wash oysters well to remove sand and grit. Prepare beds of lettuce or ice. Open oysters with oyster knife just before serving. Discard top shell; loosen oyster from bottom of shell by cutting ligaments.

Serve oysters immediately on lettuce or on ice beds. Garnish with lemon wedges; accompany with Tabasco. Pass lots of whole-wheat soda bread. Makes 4 servings.

Pickled Fish

1 **pound dressed, freshly caught whitefish**
1 **cup lime juice, freshly squeezed**
2 **tomatoes, peeled, seeded, and sliced into thin wedges**
1 **red pepper, cored, seeded, and sliced into small strips**
1 **green pepper, cored, seeded, and sliced into small strips**
¼ **cup pimiento-stuffed olives, sliced**
2 **tablespoons onion, chopped**
¼ **cup olive oil**
2 **tablespoons wine vinegar**
1 **teaspoon oregano**
1 **teaspoon salt**
½ **cup slivered blanched almonds**

Wash fish well. Remove skin or bones; slice into small pieces. Place in small glass or stainless-steel bowl. Pour lime juice over fish; refrigerate 10 to 12 hours. Spoon juice over fish every 2 hours.

Add vegetables and remaining ingredients to fish 1 hour before serving time. Toss gently. Serve fish arranged attractively on a platter with cocktail picks. Makes 8 servings.

Warm Avocado

Mousse with Smoked Herring

1	envelope gelatin	¼	teaspoon salt
3	medium smoked herrings	1	teaspoon lemon juice
1	egg	¾	cup crème fraîche or sour
¼	cup onion, minced		cream
¼	cup dill, snipped		Lettuce, shredded
⅛	teaspoon thyme		Lemon and dill for garnish

Place the gelatin in 1/4 cup cold water.

Clean the fish and finely mash up the meat, or run it through a food processor using the metal knife attachment. Mix in the egg by hand or use a food processor. Add onion and dill to the fish together with thyme, salt, and lemon juice.

Dissolve the gelatin over low heat and add the fish mixture. Finally fold in the crème fraîche or sour cream.

Pour into a mold or bowl and refrigerate so that the mousse becomes firm, about 2 hours. Spoon the mousse onto lettuce leaves and garnish with lemon and dill. Makes 4 servings.

Spiced Herring

20	medium, fresh herring (about 4½ pounds)	2	tablespoons allspice, coarsely ground
⅛	cup white vinegar	2	tablespoons black pepper, coarsely ground
4	cups water	3	tablespoons oregano
2	cups sugar	3	bay leaves, crumbled
⅓	cup coarse salt		
⅓	cup fine salt		

Clean the herrings, removing the heads but keeping the backbones. Quickly rinse the fish and let drain.

Mix vinegar and water, measuring the ingredients carefully. Place herring in a bowl, and pour the liquid over them. The pickling juice should completely cover the fish. If it does not, make more of the mixture, so that you are sure the fish lies in the juice. Place the bowl in the refrigerator for 24 hours.

After 24 hours, the meat of the fish should be completely white, all the way down to the bone. Make a cut in the back to check. If the meat is not white, let the fish stand in the juice for another 6 hours. Make sure that it is completely covered with the liquid.

Combine sugar, 2 kinds of salt, allspice, black pepper, oregano, and bay leaves. Remove herring from pickling juice and let it drain before alternating it in an earthenware pot with the spice mixture. Place something heavy over the herring so that it sinks down into the juices that are made. Let it sit for 4 to 7 days before eating it. Makes 8 servings.

Cucumber Boats

Lobster Boats

½ pound cooked lobster meat, fresh or frozen
24 fresh mushrooms, approximately 1½ inches in diameter
¼ cup condensed cream of mushroom soup
2 tablespoons fine soft bread crumbs
2 tablespoons mayonnaise or salad dressing
¼ teaspoon Worcestershire sauce
⅛ teaspoon liquid hot pepper sauce
Dash of pepper
Grated Parmesan cheese

Thaw lobster meat, if frozen. Drain lobster meat. Remove any shell or cartilage. Chop lobster meat.

Rinse mushrooms in cold water. Dry mushrooms; remove stems.

Combine soup, crumbs, mayonnaise, seasonings, and lobster. Stuff each mushroom cap with a tablespoonful of lobster mixture. Sprinkle with cheese.

Place mushrooms on well-buttered, 15 × 10 × 1-inch baking pan. Bake in 400°F oven 10 to 15 minutes or until lightly browned. Makes 24 hors d'oeuvres.

Luxury Toast

4 slices white bread
1 (9-ounce) can asparagus
Butter
About 1 pound shrimp, preferably frozen
2 egg whites
2 tablespoons chili sauce
4 tablespoons mayonnaise
Lettuce leaves
Sprigs of dill

Fry slices of white bread in lightly browned butter until they are crisp and golden brown on both sides. Allow them to cool. Pour off asparagus juice. Make sure asparagus are well drained. Divide up asparagus betwen slices of bread, placing 2 rows of double asparagus on each slice. Shell shrimp and divide them between bread slices so that they seem to "ride" on top of the asparagus.

Beat egg whites into unusually stiff peaks. Blend chili sauce with mayonnaise before carefully folding this mixture into egg whites. Spread egg mixture over shrimp and asparagus so that they are totally covered. Immediately bake the sandwiches at 400°F until the mayonnaise soufflé has risen and become golden brown.

Serve immediately, garnished with lettuce and dill sprigs. Makes 4 servings.

Cucumber Cheese Barrels

Party Salmon Ball

1	(1-pound) can salmon	1	teaspoon prepared
8	ounces cream cheese,		horseradish
	room temperature	¼	teaspoon salt
1	tablespoon lemon juice	3	drops liquid smoke
2	teaspoons onion, grated	½	cup pecans, chopped

Drain salmon thoroughly; flake carefully with fork or your fingers. Combine salmon with softened cream cheese. Add next 5 ingredients; mix thoroughly. Cover bowl. Refrigerate a few hours, until firm.

Shape salmon into ball; roll in nuts. Wrap tightly in plastic wrap; return to refrigerator until serving. Serve with firm, unflavored crackers. Makes 10 to 12 cocktail appetizers.

Seafood Cocktail

1 orange
2 tablespoons kirsch
12 blue grapes, halved and
   seeds discarded
Lettuce leaves
1 small can white asparagus
   tips (optional; available in
   specialty food stores)
12 ounces canned or cooked
   seafood (shrimp, lobster,
   scallops, or crab meat)

Cocktail Dressing
¼ cup mayonnaise
¼ cup plain yogurt

1 teaspoon catsup
1 teaspoon prepared
   horseradish
Freshly ground black pepper
   to taste
Few drops Worcestershire
   sauce, to taste
1 tablespoon lemon juice
Salt and pepper to taste

Garnishes
Whole blue grapes
Unpeeled orange slices, halved
Cooked crab claws

Peel orange; remove as much white membrane as possible. Cut into slices and each slice into quarters. Sprinkle with kirsch.

Prepare dressing by blending together all dressing ingredients. Arrange orange pieces in 4 champagne glasses lined with lettuce leaves. Add grape halves and asparagus tips. Arrange selected seafood on top. Pour dressing over all.

Serve seafood cocktail at once, garnished with whole grapes, half slice of unpeeled orange, and a crab claw. Makes 4 servings.

Shrimp and Mushroom Cocktail

¼ cup long-grain rice
1 small (10-ounce) package
   frozen peas
¼ pound shrimp (fresh,
   canned or frozen)
1 (7½-ounce) can button
   mushrooms

1 red-skinned eating apple
1 teaspoon lemon juice
1 tablespoon parsley,
   chopped
2 tablespoons mayonnaise
8 lettuce leaves, shredded
4 twists of lemon for garnish

Cook rice in a pan of boiling salted water for 10 to 15 minutes. Drain and cool. Cook peas according to instructions on package. Drain and cool. Mix cooled rice and peas with all remaining ingredients except lettuce.

Divide shredded lettuce between 4 individual glasses or dishes. Place shrimp filling on top. Garnish each cocktail with a twist of lemon. Chill before serving. Serve with melba toast. Makes 4 servings.

Leeks with Mustard Greens and Cress

Shrimp Balls

1 medium onion, grated	1 medium raw potato, grated
1½ pounds raw shrimp, shelled, deveined, and grated	1 egg, slightly beaten
	Salt and pepper to taste
	Fat for deep frying

Grind or grate onion and shrimp into large bowl. Grind potato; pat dry with paper towel. Stir in egg, salt, and pepper. Potato is the thickening; batter will be thick.

Heat deep fat; drop batter in by spoonfuls. Fry until golden brown; remove with slotted spoon. Drain on paper towels. Serve hot. Makes 36 to 48 shrimp balls.

Shrimp Tree

3 pounds shrimp, fresh or frozen	1 styrofoam cone, 2½ feet high
2 quarts water	1 small box round toothpicks
½ cup salt	
4 large bunches curly endive	

Thaw shrimp if frozen. Place shrimp in boiling salted water; cover. Simmer about 5 minutes or until shrimp are pink and tender; drain. Peel shrimp. Remove sand veins; wash. Chill.

Separate and wash endive; chill.

Fasten endive to styrofoam cone with toothpick halves. Start at outside edge of base; work up. Cover fully with greens to resemble tree. Attach shrimp artistically to tree with toothpicks.

Place tree on large plate or tray; add leftover shrimp around base. Top tree with ribbon, tinsel, or your favorite ornament. Provide cocktail sauce for dunking.

You can keep a bowl of prepared shrimp in the refrigerator and replenish tree as needed. Yield as desired.

Mushroom Toast with Garlic

Radish Crowns

Vegetable Appetizers

Cucumber Boats

1	cucumber	2	hard-boiled eggs
1	(4½-ounce) can sardines	1	level teaspoon salt
½	cup mayonnaise	½	level teaspoon pepper
2	teaspoons lemon juice	1	lettuce
1	level tablespoon parsley, chopped	½	head celery
		2	large carrots

Cut cucumber into 2-1/2 inch lengths. Cut in half lengthwise, remove 1/2 inch strip of skin underneath cucumber pieces to make them stand up. Cut each strip into 2 triangles to make sails. Remove soft center from each piece of cucumber.

Drain sardines and mash them in a bowl with mayonnaise and lemon juice. Chop parsley and hard-boiled eggs, add them to sardine mixture with salt and pepper. Fill cucumber pieces with mixture.

Arrange the cucumbers on a serving plate. Shred lettuce; cut celery into 1-inch pieces and carrot into wedges. Arrange these vegetables on serving plate in between the cucumber boats. Secure sails by pushing narrow end of the sail into the filling and propping it up with a cocktail stick if necessary. Makes 8 servings.

Cucumber Cheese Barrels

1 cucumber	2 tablespoons mayonnaise
1 (8-ounce) package cream cheese	Salt and pepper
	Radishes for garnish
1 to 2 teaspoons curry powder	

Wipe cucumber with a damp cloth and divide into 8 pieces. Make a slight indentation in top of each piece, using a teaspoon to remove some of the flesh.

Mix cream cheese, curry powder, mayonnaise and seasoning. Place in a piping bag, fitted with a large star tube, and pipe cheese filling on top of each cucumber barrel. Slice radishes and use as garnish. Makes 4 servings.

Stuffed Mushrooms

4 large or 8 smaller mushrooms	½ small red pepper
	¼ cup cooked ham, chopped
4 tablespoons margarine	1 level tablespoon parsley, chopped
1 small onion, chopped	
1 tablespoon flour	Salt and pepper
½ cup milk	⅓ cup fresh bread crumbs

Wipe mushrooms, remove stalks, and reserve. Put mushroom caps, upside down, in a shallow, greased, ovenproof dish. Dot with 2 tablespoons of margarine and bake in a 350°F oven for 10 minutes.

Meanwhile, heat remaining margarine in a saucepan and fry onion until softened. Stir in flour and cook, stirring, for 2 to 3 minutes. Blend in milk and bring to a boil, stirring all the time. Boil for 2 minutes.

Chop reserved mushroom stalks and half the pepper (slice remainder of the pepper for garnish). Add pepper, mushroom stalks, ham, parsley, salt, pepper, and bread crumbs to sauce. Pile some stuffing into each mushroom cap. Return to oven and bake for a further 15 to 20 minutes. Serve hot, garnished with strips of red pepper. Serve as a first course or as an appetizer. Makes 4 servings.

Seafood Stuffed Mushrooms

8	ounces cooked crab, shrimp, or lobster, minced	1	teaspoon cornstarch
4	water chestnuts, minced	1	egg
1	scallion, minced	12	mushroom stems, minced and browned in a little oil
2	teaspoons soy sauce	12	large mushrooms, stems removed
1	teaspoon dry sherry		Parsley (optional)
1	teaspoon sugar		

Combine all ingredients except mushroom caps and parsley. Fill mushroom caps with mixture. Bake at 350°F 20 minutes. Serve hot, garnished with parsley. Allow 2 or 3 to a person for a first course, or use smaller mushrooms, and serve on melba rounds as finger food. Makes 12 appetizers.

Mushroom and Onion Quiche

	Pastry for single-crust 9-inch pie	2	eggs
3	tablespoons butter or margarine	½	can evaporated milk (about 1 cup)
2	onions, peeled and chopped	½	cup grated cheese
1	can button mushrooms (about 1 cup)		Pinch of dry mustard

Preheat oven to 400°F. Line deep 8-inch pie plate with pastry.

Heat 2 tablespoons butter in frying pan; cook onion until transparent. Drain well; put into pastry shell with most of mushrooms, cut in halves. Leave a few uncut for decoration.

Beat eggs; stir in evaporated milk, grated cheese, and seasoning. Pour over mushrooms. Bake about 35 minutes.

Sauté remaining mushrooms a few minutes in 1 tablespoon butter. Drain; cut into thin slices.

When pie is cooked, decorate with sliced mushrooms. Makes 4 to 5 servings.

Mushroom Toast with Garlic

24 fine, white mushrooms	2 tablespoons parsley, chopped
1 lemon	Salt
7 tablespoons butter, at room temperature	Pepper
3 cloves garlic, crushed	6 slices white bread, crusts removed
1 tablespoon shallot, finely chopped	

Clean mushrooms and drip a small amount of lemon juice over them so that they stay white.

Mix butter with garlic, shallot, parsley, and juice from 1/2 lemon. Add salt and pepper to taste.

Fry bread until golden brown on one side. Cut mushrooms into thin slices and place them on unfried side of the bread. Cover with butter mixture and place in the oven under the broiler. Serve when the butter has started to become brown on the top. Makes 6 servings.

Leeks with Mustard Greens and Cress

1 pound small leeks	*Dressing*
Water	1 tablespoon vinegar
Salt	½ teaspoon salt
Mustard greens and cress	½ teaspoon tarragon
	1 tablespoon water
	1 teaspoon mustard
	3 to 4 tablespoons oil

Wash leeks well and trim root ends and most of the green. In a wide, shallow pan, bring water to a boil, adding 2 teaspoons salt per quart of water. Divide leeks into 2 or 3 pieces, if they are very long. Cook for about 2 minutes, depending on thickness. Do not overcook.

Blend ingredients for the dressing and beat for a few minutes to allow salt to dissolve. Drain leeks and place in a dish. Pour dressing over them while they are still hot. Allow them to get cold and marinate for an hour or 2. Cut some mustard greens and cress onto the leeks when serving and offer bread and butter with them. Makes 4 servings.

Vegetable Fritters

Stuffed Zucchini Hors d'Oeuvres

3 small zucchini, unpeeled	1 clove garlic, minced
4 ounces cream cheese, softened	1 teaspoon parsley, chopped
3 slices bacon, crisped and crumbled	¼ teaspoon black pepper

Cut off zucchini ends; scoop out centers with long-handled spoon. Mix remaining ingredients together. Stuff mixture firmly into center of zucchini, using a pastry bag with a wide-mouthed tip or a small spoon; chill. To serve, cut into 1/2-inch slices. Makes 4 to 6 servings.

Warm Avocado

4 small eggs	3½ tablespoons butter
4 cups water	Pinch salt
2 teaspoons salt	Tarragon, finely crushed
1 teaspoon vinegar	Snipped parsley
1 egg yolk	2 large, ripe avocados
1 teaspoon lemon juice	Juice from ½ lemon
1 tablespoon cream	

Start by poaching the eggs. Break each egg into its own cup. Combine water, salt, and vinegar and bring to a boil. Lift from the heat and let 1 egg slide out of the cup into the water. Fold the egg white that spreads out into the water back to the egg with a spoon. Cook the egg carefully for about 4 to 5 minutes, so that the egg white becomes firm. Do only 1 egg at a time. Remove the egg from the water, using a large spoon with holes in it. Trim the egg with a pair of scissors so that it has an even edge and looks attractive. It should not be larger than the hole from the seed in the avocado half. Keep the eggs warm by placing over 98.6°F water next to the stove.

Mix egg yolk, lemon juice, and cream in a small saucepan (it should not be an aluminum pan). Carefully warm over low direct heat while stirring constantly. Lift the pan every now and then from the burner so that it doesn't become too warm. As soon as the mixture starts to foam or thicken, add the butter in small dabs while continuing to beat constantly. Beat until the sauce is thick and light and all the butter has been added. Remove from the heat and season with salt, finely crushed tarragon, and a little snipped parsley. Keep warm by placing it in 98.6°F water next to the stove.

Divide avocados in half, remove seeds, and dig out a slightly larger hole using a spoon. Place avocado halves in a skillet. Pour in warm water so that it just covers avocados and add lemon juice. Bring slowly to a boil without covering pan. Remove avocados with a spoon that has holes in it so that the water drains off; place each of the 4 halves on a warm plate.

Pour a little of the sauce into each hole. Also place a poached egg into each of the holes, then cover the eggs with the rest of the sauce. Makes 4 servings.

Stuffed Mushrooms

Radish Crowns

6 ounces cream cheese	Pinch of mixed dried herbs
4 tablespoons margarine	4 slices bread
½ level teaspoon salt	6 radishes, thinly sliced
½ level teaspoon pepper	

Place cream cheese in a bowl, blend in 2 tablespoons of margarine, salt, pepper, and herbs with a wooden spoon until well mixed. Place mixture in a piping bag with a large star pipe. Cut each slice of bread into 4, 1-inch rounds.

Heat remaining margarine in a frying pan and fry rounds of bread on both sides until golden brown. Drain on paper towels and leave to cool. Pipe rosettes of the creamed mixture onto bread rounds and garnish with slices of radish as shown in the picture. Makes 16 crowns.

Vegetable Fritters

1 small eggplant	¾ cup flour
Salt	2 eggs
1 large zucchini	4 tablespoons milk
½ small cauliflower	Oil for deep-frying

Slice eggplant into thin rounds. Place slices in a colander and sprinkle with salt. Cover with a plate and put aside for 30 minutes. Slice zucchini. Divide cauliflower into flowerets.

Sift flour into a mixing bowl with a pinch of salt. Make a well in the center and add eggs. Mix eggs into flour; gradually add milk, beating well until batter is smooth. Rinse then drain eggplant and pat dry with paper towels. Fill a deep frying pan half full of oil. When fat is hot, dip vegetables into batter and fry individual pieces until golden all over. Drain on paper towels and serve as soon as possible. Makes 6 servings.

Stuffed Olives

1 (6-ounce) can jumbo
  pitted black olives
1 (2-ounce) can anchovy
  fillets
2 tablespoons olive oil
1 clove garlic, minced

2 tablespoons parsley, finely
  chopped
12 stemmed cherry tomatoes
½ of medium green pepper,
  thinly sliced

Drain olives. Drain anchovy fillets; cut each in half. Stuff each olive with half an anchovy fillet. Place in serving bowl.

Combine olive oil, garlic, and parsley; pour over olives. Mix well. Chill several hours. Bring to room temperature before serving.

Garnish with cherry tomatoes and green peppers. Provide cocktail picks for guests to spear these. Makes 6 servings.

EQUIVALENT MEASURES

dash = 2 or 3 drops
pinch = amount that can be held
            between ends of thumb &
            forefinger
1 tablespoon = 3 teaspoons
¼ cup = 4 tablespoons
⅓ cup = 5 tablespoons + 1 teaspoon
½ cup = 8 tablespoons
1 cup = 16 tablespoons
1 pint = 2 cups
1 quart = 4 cups
1 gallon = 4 quarts
1 peck = 8 quarts
1 bushel = 4 pecks
1 pound = 16 ounces

KITCHEN METRIC

measurements you will encounter
most often in recipes are: centimeter
(cm), milliliter (ml), gram (g),
kilogram (kg)

cup equivalents (volume):

    ¼   cup = 60 ml
    ⅓   cup = 85 ml
    ½   cup = 125 ml
    ⅔   cup = 170 ml
    ¾   cup = 180 ml
    1   cup = 250 ml
    1¼ cups = 310 ml
    1½ cups = 375 ml
    2   cups = 500 ml
    3   cups = 750 ml
    5   cups = 1250 ml

spoonful equivalents (volume):

    ⅛   teaspoon = .5 ml
    ¼   teaspoon = 1.5 ml
    ½   teaspoon = 3 ml
    ¾   teaspoon = 4 ml
    1   teaspoon = 5 ml
    1   tablespoon = 15 ml
    2   tablespoons = 30 ml
    3   tablespoons = 45 ml

pan sizes (linear & volume):

    1 inch = 2.5 cm
    8-inch square = 20-cm square
    9 × 13 × 1½-inch = 20 × 33 × 4-cm
    10 × 6 × 2-inch = 25 × 15 × 5-cm
    13 × 9 × 2-inch = 33 × 23 × 5-cm
    7½ × 12 × 1½-inch = 18 × 30 × 4-cm
    (above are baking dishes, pans)
    9 × 5 × 3-inch = 23 × 13 × 8-cm
    (loaf pan)
    10-inch = 25 cm   12-inch = 30-cm
    (skillets)
    1-quart = 1-liter   2-quart = 2-liter
    (baking dishes, by volume)
    5- to 6-cup = 1.5-liter
    (ring mold)

weight (meat amounts;
can & package sizes):

    1   ounce = 28 g
    ½   pound = 225 g
    ¾   pound = 340 g
    1   pound = 450 g
    1½   pounds = 675 g
    2   pounds = 900 g
    3   pounds = 1.4 kg (in recipes,
          amounts of meat above 2 pounds
          will generally be stated in
          kilograms)
    10   ounces = 280 g
          (most frozen vegetables)
    10½ ounces = 294 g
          (most condensed soups)
    15   ounces = 425 g
          (common can size)
    16   ounces = 450 g
          (common can size)
    1   pound, 24 ounces = 850 g
          (can size)

OVEN TEMPERATURES

275°F = 135°C
300°F = 149°C
325°F = 165°C
350°F = 175°C
375°F = 190°C
400°F = 205°C
425°F = 218°C
450°F = 230°C
500°F = 260°C

Note that Celsius temperatures are
sometimes rounded off to the nearest
reading ending in 0 or 5; the Celsius
thermometer is the same as
Centigrade, a term no longer used.

Index

Almonds, Salted, 68
Apple Soup, Danish, 13
Asparagus Soup, Cold, 32
Avocado
 Dip, 70
 Soup, 33
 Warm, 90

Bacon Croutons, 11
Bean(s)
 Soup, Brown, 32
 Soup, Green, 30
Beef
 Shank Supper Soup, 16
 Stock, 6
 Zorn Soup, 54
Beef, Ground
 Meatballs, Cocktail, 64
 Meatballs, Swedish, 64
Beet Soup, Cold, with Sour Cream, 34
Bouillabaisse, Quick, 28
Broccoli
 Soup, Cream of, 36
 Soup, Creamy Crab, 26

Cabbage Soup, 36
Carrot Soup, 37
Cauliflower Cream Soup, 34
Celery and Walnut Soup, 38
Cheese
 Appetizers, Bacon and, 56
 Cheddar Puffs, 56
 Crisps, 55
 Croutons, 9
 Fried Profiteroles, 56
 Mold, 57
 Soup, 14
 Turnovers, Greek Spinach and, 58
Cherry Soup, Swiss, 12
Chicken
 Gumbo, 20

and Ham Soup, 18
 Pâté Cream, 62
 Soup, Cream of, 20
 Soup, Giblet, 22
 Stock, 6
Clam(s)
 Chowder, New England, 28
 Dip, Clamdigger, 72
 Stuffed, 73
Cod Soup with Orange, 26
Corn
 Chowder, Old-Fashioned, 40
 Soup, Cream of, 38
Crab
 Balls, 74
 Dabs, 74
 Soup, Creamy Broccoli, 26
 Soup, Maryland, 25
Croissants, Party, 60
Croutons
 Bacon, 11
 Cheese, 9
 Fried Bread, 11
Cucumber
 Boats, 85
 Cheese Barrels, 86
 Soup, Chilled, 41
Curry Dip, Creamy, 70

Eggs, Stuffed, 59

Fish
 Neapolitan Chowder, 29
 Pickled, 75
 Stock, 7

Garden Dip, 72
Goulash Soup, 18
Greek Lemon Soup, 14
Green Bean Soup, 30

Herring
  Smoked, Mousse with, 76
  Spiced, 76

Kebabs, Oriental Cocktail, 66

Leeks with Mustard Greens and Cress,
  88
Lentil
  Soup, 41
  Soup, Red and Green, 42
Liver Pâté, Party, 63
Lobster Boats, 78
Luxury Toast, 78

Meatballs
  Cocktail, 64
  Swedish, 64
Mushroom(s)
  Cocktail, Shrimp and, 80
  Quiche, and Onion, 87
  Seafood Stuffed, 87
  Soup, Cream of, 42
  Soup, Fresh, 42
  Stuffed, 86
  Toast with Garlic, 88

Nuts
  Almonds, Salted, 68
  Curried, 68

Olives, Stuffed, 93
Onion Party Dip, 69
Onion Soup, 44
Orange
  Cups, Cottage, 61
  Soup, 14
Oxtail Soup, 24
Oysters on the Half Shell, 74

Pâté
  Chicken Cream, 62
  Liver, Party, 63
Pavian Soup, 21
Pea Soup with Ham, 44
Peanut Soup, 46
Pigs in Blankets, 66

Potato(es)
  Soup, 46
  Soup, Green, 47

Radish Crowns, 92

Salmon Ball, Party, 79
Seafood Cocktail, 80
Seafood Stuffed Mushrooms, 87
Sherry Bisque, 48
Shrimp
  Balls, 82
  Cocktail, and Mushroom, 80
  Dip, 72
  Luxury Toast, 78
  Soup, Savory, 27
  Tree, 82
Spinach
  Soup, 48
  Turnovers, and Cheese, Greek, 58
Spring Soup, 50
Squash Soup, Winter, 50
Stock
  Beef, 6
  Brown, 5
  Chicken, 6
  Fish, 7
  Vegetable, 8
  White, 8

Tomato
  Soup, and Vegetable, Cold, 51
  Soup, Clear, 49
Turkey Soup, and Chestnut, 22

Vegetable
  Chowder, New England, 52
  Fritters, 92
  Soup, and Tomato, Cold, 51
  Stock, 8

Watercress Soup, 52
White Stock, 8

Yarmouth Straws, 60

Zorn Soup, 54
Zucchini Hors d'Oeuvres, 89